Communications in Computer and Information Science   1670

More information about this series at https://link.springer.com/bookseries/7899

Costin Badica · Marcin Paprzycki ·
Latika Kharb · Deepak Chahal (Eds.)

Information, Communication and Computing Technology

7th International Conference, ICICCT 2022
New Delhi, India, July 16, 2022
Revised Selected Papers

 Springer

Editors
Costin Badica (iD)
University of Craiova
Craiova, Romania

Marcin Paprzycki (iD)
Systems Research Institute
Warsaw, Poland

Latika Kharb (iD)
Jagan Institute of Management Studies
Delhi, India

Deepak Chahal (iD)
Jagan Institute of Management Studies
Delhi, India

ISSN 1865-0929 ISSN 1865-0937 (electronic)
Communications in Computer and Information Science
ISBN 978-3-031-20976-5 ISBN 978-3-031-20977-2 (eBook)
https://doi.org/10.1007/978-3-031-20977-2

This Springer imprint is published by the registered company Springer Nature Switzerland AG
The registered company address is: Gewerbestrasse 11, 6330 Cham, Switzerland

Preface

The International Conference on Information, Communication and Computing Technology (ICICCT 2022) was held on July 16, 2022 in New Delhi, India. ICICCT 2022 was organized by the Department of Information Technology, Jagan Institute of Management Studies (JIMS) Rohini, New Delhi, India. The conference received 220 submissions and after rigorous reviews, 11 papers were selected for this volume. The acceptance rate was around 16.9%. The contributions came from diverse areas of Information technology categorized into two tracks, namely (1) Networking and Communication and (2) Evolutionary Computing through Machine Learning.

The aim of ICICCT 2022 was to provide a global platform for researchers, scientists and practitioners from both academia and industry to present their research and development activities in all the aspects of communication and network systems and computational Intelligence techniques.

We thank all the members of the Organizing Committee and the Program Committee for their hard work. We are very grateful to Marcin Paprzycki, Associate Professor, Systems Research Institute, Polish Academy of Sciences, Poland as General Chair, Milan Simic, RMIT University, Australia as the first keynote speaker, Jean Paul Van Belle, Professor and Director, Centre for Information Technology and National Development, University of Cape Town, Africa as the second keynote speaker. Subrata Nandi, Professor, Department of Computer Science Engineering, National Institute of Technology, Durgapur, India as session chair for Track 1, Namita Mittal, Associate Professor, Department of Computer Science Engineering, Malaviya National Institute of Technology, Jaipur, India as session chair for Track 2.

We thank all the Technical Program Committee members and referees for their constructive and enlightening reviews on the manuscripts. We thank Springer for publishing the proceedings in the Communications in Computer and Information Science (CCIS) series. We thank all the authors and participants for their great contributions that made this conference possible.

August 2022

Costin Badica
Latika Kharb
Deepak Chahal

Organization

General Chair

Marcin Paprzycki — Systems Research Institute, Polish Academy of Sciences, Poland

Program Chair

Costin Badica — University of Craiova, Romania

Keynote Speakers

Milan Simic — RMIT University, Australia
Jean Paul Van Belle — University of Cape Town, Africa

International Advisory Chair

Maria Ganzha — Warsaw University of Technology, Poland

Conference Secretariat

Praveen Arora — Jagan Institute of Management Studies, India

Session Chair for Track 1

Subrata Nandi — National Institute of Technology, Durgapur, India

Session Chair for Track 2

Namita Mittal — National Institute of Technology, Jaipur, India

Convener

Latika Kharb — Jagan Institute of Management Studies, India
Deepak Chahal — Jagan Institute of Management Studies, India

Technical Program Committee

Jarrod Trevathan	Griffith University, Australia
Saim Rasheed	King Abdulaziz University, Saudi Arabia
Shangqing Zhao	University of Oklahoma, USA
Saaidal Razalli	University of Malaya, Malaysia
Mohammed Moshiul Hoque	Chittagong University of Engineering and Technology, Bangladesh
Ali J. Abboud	University of Diyala, Baqubah, Iraq
R. S. Ponmagal	SRM Institute of Science and Technology, India
Boudhir Anouar Abdelhakim	Abdelmalek Essaâdi University, Morocco
Nikhil Marriwala	Kurukshetra University, India
Ghada Alamoudi	King Abdulaziz University, Saudi Arabia
Janmenjoy Nayak	Maharaja Sriram Chandra Bhanja Deo University, India
Hasan Al-Marzouqi	Khalifa University, Abu Dhabi, United Arab Emirates
Surbhi Gupta	Punjab Agricultural University, India
Ahmad T. Al-Taani	Princess Sumaya University for Technology, Jordan
Chakchai So-In	Khon Kaen University, Thailand
HyunSeok Park	Ewha Womans University, South Korea
Jasminder Kaur Sandhu	Chitkara University, India
Richard C. Millham	Durban University of Technology, South Africa
Mohammad Ashrafuzzaman Khan	North South University, Bangladesh
D. Malathi	SRM Institute of Science and Technology, India
Asma Cherif	King Abdulaziz University, Saudi Arabia
Sharanjit Kaur	Acharya Narendra Dev College, India
Zati Azizul	University of Malaya, Malaysia
Imad Ahmed Shaheen	University College of Science and Technology, Palestine
Baha' A. Alsaify	Jordan University of Science and Technology, Jordan
Rastislav Roka	Slovak University of Technology, Slovakia
Siddhivinayak Kulkarni	MIT World Peace University, India
P. Chenna Reddy	Jawaharlal Nehru Technological University, India
Rakesh Kumar Mandal	University of North Bengal, India
Razali Yaakob	University Putra, Malaysia
Saad Al-Azawi	University of Diyala, Iraq
Zareen Alamgir	National University of Computer and Emerging Sciences, Pakistan
Ali Kadhum Idrees	University of Babylon, Iraq
Praveen Kumar Malik	Lovely Professional University, India

Kofi Sarpong Adu-Manu	Valley View University, Ghana
Chaw Seng Woo	University of Malaya, Malaysia
Yusliza Yusoff	University of Technology Malaysia, Malaysia
Noor Afiza Mohd Ariffin	Universiti Putra Malaysia, Malaysia
M. Babu Reddy	Krishna University, India
Ohoud Alzamzami	King Abdulaziz University, Jeddah, Saudi Arabia
Pang Yee Yong	University of Technology Malaysia, Malaysia
Roselina Sallehuddin	University of Technology Malaysia, Malaysia
Ahmad Khan	COMSATS University Islamabad, Pakistan
Mohd Abdul Ahad	Jamia Hamdard, India
Zuriahati binti Mohd Yunos	University of Malaya, Kuala Lumpur, Malaysia
Siti Zaiton Mohd Hashim	Universiti Teknologi Malaysia, Malaysiachan
Shahab Shamshirband	Iran University of Science and Technology, Iran
Atul Gonsai Gosai	Saurashtra University, India
Kumaratharan N.	Sri Venkateswara College of Engineering, Tamil Nadu, India
Shamimul Qamar	King Khalid University, Saudi Arabia
P. Subashini Avinashilingam	Avinashilingam Institute for Home Science and Higher Education for Women, India
Abdullah Basuhail	King Abdulaziz University, Saudi Arabia
Sim Hiew Moi	University of Malaya, Kuala Lumpur, Malaysia
Azurah A. Samah	University of Malaya, Kuala Lumpur, Malaysia
C. Shoba Bindu	JNTUA College of Engineering, India
S. Pallam Setty	Andra University, India
K. Madhavi	JNTUA College of Engineering, India
Janaka Wijekoon	Sri Lanka Institute of Information Technology, Sri Lanka
Hanumanthappa. J.	University of Mysore, India
K. Thabotharan	University of Jaffna, Sri Lanka
Izyan Izzati Kamsani	University of Malaya, Kuala Lumpur, Malaysia
Kamal Eldahshan	Al-Azhar University, Egypt
Tony Smith	University of Waikato, New Zealand
K. Lakshmi Narayanan	Francis Xavier Engineering College,India
Abdel-Badeeh Salem	Ain Shams University, Egypt
Khalid Nazim Sattar Abdul	Majmaah University, Saudi Arabia
H. S. Nagendraswamy	University of Mysore, India
Wathiq Laftah Al-Yaseen	Al-Furat Al-Awsat Technical University, Iraq
S. R. Boselin Prabhu	Anna University, India
S. Rajalakshmi	Sri Chandrasekharendra Saraswathi Viswa Mahavidyalaya, India
Anastasios Politis	Technological and Educational Institute of Central Macedonia, Greece

Subhash Chandra Yadav	Central University of Jharkhand, India
Uttam Ghosh	Vanderbilt University, USA
Wafaa Shalash	King Abdulaziz University, Saudi Arabia
Etimad Fadel	King Abdulaziz University, Saudi Arabia
Oleksii Tyshchenko	University of Ostrava, Czech Republic
Hima Bindu Maringanti	Maharaja Sriram Chandra Bhanja Deo University, India
Latafat A. Gardashova	Azerbaijan State Oil Academy, Azerbaijan
Wenjian Hu	Meta, USA
Vinoth Babu Kumaravelu	Vellore Institute of Technology, Tamil Nadu, India
Muhammad Umair Ramzan	King Abdulaziz University, Saudi Arabia
Areej Abbas Malibary	King Abdulaziz University, Saudi Arabia
P. R. Patil	PSGVP Mandal's D.N.Patel College of Engineering, India
Jose Neuman Souza	Federal University of Ceara, Brazil
Nermin Hamza	King Abdulaziz University, Saudi Arabia
R. Chithra	K.S. Rangasamy College of Technology, India
Homero Toral Cruz	University of Quintana Roo, Mexico
J. Viji Gripsy	SGR Krishnammal College for Women, Coimbatore, India
Boudhir Anouar Abdelhakim	Abdelmalek Essaâdi University, UAE
Muhammed Ali Aydin	Istanbul Cerrahpaşa University, Turkey
Suhair Alshehri	King Abdulaziz University, Saudi Arabia
Dalibor Dobrilovic	University of Novi Sad, Serbia
A. V. Petrashenko	National Technical University of Ukraine, Ukraine
Ali Hussain	Sri Sai Madhari Institute of Science and Technology, India
A. NagaRaju	Central University of Rajasthan, India
Cheng-Chi Lee	Fu Jen Catholic University, Taiwan
Apostolos Gkamas	University Ecclesiastical Academy of Vella of Ioannina, Greece
M. A. H. Akhand	Khulna University of Engineering and Technology, Bangladesh
Saad Talib Hasson	University of Babylon, Iraq
Valeri Mladenov	Technical University of Sofia, Bulgaria
Kate Revoredo	Humboldt University of Berlin, Germany
Dimitris Kanellopoulos	University of Patras, Greece
Samir Kumar Bandyopadhyay	University of Calcutta, India
Baljit Singh Khehra	BBSBEC, India
Md Gapar Md Johar	Management Science University, Malaysia
Kathemreddy Ramesh Reddy	Vikrama Simhapuri University, India
Shubhnandan Singh Jamwa	University of Jammu, India

Surjeet Dalal	SRM Institute of Science and Technology, India
Faisal K. Shaikh	Mehran University of Engineering and Technology, Pakistan
Adeyemi Ikuesan	University of Pretoria, South Africa
Pinaki Chakraborty	Netaji Subhas University of Technology, India
Subrata Nandi	National Institute of Technology, Durgapur, India
Vinod Keshaorao Pachghare	College of Engineering, Pune, India
A. V. Senthil Kumar	Hindusthan College of Arts and Science, India
Khalid Raza	Jamia Milia Islamia, Delhi, India
G. Vijaya Lakshmi	Vikrama Simhapuri University, Nellore, India
Parameshachari B. D.	GSSS Institute of Engineering and Technology for Women, India
Subalalitha C. N.	SRM Institute of Science and Technology India
T. Sobha Rani	University of Hyderabad, India
Zunnun Narmawala	Nirma University, India
Aniruddha Chandra	National Institute of Technology Durgapur, India
Ashwani Kush	Kurukshetra University, India
Manoj Sahni	Pandit Deendayal Petroleum University, India
Promila Bahadur	Maharishi University of Management, USA
Gajendra Sharma	Kathmandu University, Nepal
Doukha Zouina	University of Science and Technology, Algeria
Eduard Babulak	Institute of Technology and Business, Czech Republic
Zoran Bojkovic	University of Belgrade, Serbia
Pradeep Tomar	Gautam Buddha University, India
Arvind Selwal	Central University of Jammu, India
Atif. Farid. Mohammad	University of North Carolina at Charlotte, USA
Maushumi Barooah	Assam Engineering College, Guwahati, India
D. Davronbekov	Tashkent University of Information Technologies, Uzbekistan
J. Vijayakumar	Bharathiar University, Coimbatore, India
Jacek Izydorczyk	Silesian University of Technology, Poland
Pamela L. Thompson	University of North Carolina at, Charlotte, USA
Arka Prokash Mazumdar	Malaviya National Institute of Technology Jaipur, India
Dhiah Al-Shammary	University of Al-Qadisiyah, Iraq
Nitin Kumar	National Institute of Technology Uttarakhand, India
Manas Ranjan Kabat	VSS University of Technology, Burla, India
Md. Alimul Haque	Veer Kunwar Singh University, India
Abdullah M. Al BinAli	Taibah University, Saudi Arabia
Subhojit Ghosh	National Institute of Technology Raipur, India

Contents

Networking and Communication

Energy Efficient Communication Using Constrained Application Protocol for IoT Devices

Namrata Singh[✉] [ID] and Ayan Kumar Das [ID]

Birla Institute of Technology, Mesra, Patna Campus, Patna 800014, India
{phdcs10061.20,das.ayan}@bitmesra.ac.in

Abstract. IoT communication protocols are the integral part for device-to-device communication in an IoT environment. It enables physical devices to exchange information in a structured and meaningful way. CoAP is mainly designed for the power-constrained IoT devices, which provides the resource discovery mechanism to update the Resource Directory (RD) periodically. The centralized mode of resource discovery enables the RD to host and maintain the update information of every resource under the predefined domain and can respond to the requests on behalf of any node. To the best of our knowledge the issue of duplicate updates to RD in a periodic update environment is a major concern and still an untouched area to researchers. Number of duplicate updates highly affects the battery lifetime. Various researches have been performed to focus either on interval tuning or change in data readings to improve power consumption behavior. In this paper, the proposed dynamic update interval tunning algorithm is the hybrid form of interval tuning and change in data reading that uses the concept of alternate odd and even type of update. It reduces the number of duplicate updates as well as solve the issues of dead node condition and long waiting time of RD too. The experimental analysis shows that the proposed dynamic update interval tuning approach extends the battery lifetime to 70% and outperforms dynamic power tuning and adaptive fibonacci-based interval tuning approaches.

Keywords: Internet of Things · Internet protocol · CoAP · Resource directory · Update interval tuning · Power consumption

1 Introduction

The Internet of Things (IoT) is the network of connected objects such as variety of smart devices, technologies, and applications communicating over the internet with machine-to-machine interaction. It is rapidly gaining a vast attention of researchers with the aim to improve the quality of human life by converting the present reality into smart virtual technologies [13]. IoT protocols help to establish communication among IoT devices, cloud-based server and other applications over the Internet. It helps to send commands to IoT device and receive data from an IoT device over the internet [1].

The term 'Internet' refers to the global interconnectivity of computer networks using the standard suite of communication protocols such as Transmission Control Protocol/Internet Protocol (TCP/IP) and User Datagram Protocol (UDP) that provides worldwide services to the users. IP is the primary communication protocol that establishes the network connections over the internet. Each data packet is addressed individually to transmit it from source to destination and no acknowledgement of this transmission is sent to the source. It confirms that IP does not provide packet ordering and error checking mechanism. TCP works well with the IP in order to establish connection between source and destination with ordered transmission by providing sequencing and segmentation of data packet. TCP provides acknowledgement feature for a transmission and data flow is managed through flow control process. UDP works similar to the TCP except error checking and correction procedure and it throws out all the back and forth communications. It results in reduction of overhead in protocol stack. UDP is best suited for the time-constrained environments where speed is most desirable. IP is network layer protocol that supports both the protocols of transport layer i.e., TCP and UDP. IP is used in two versions: IPv4 and IPv6. Demand of IPv6 is growing as it provides significantly high IP addresses as compared to IPv4. IPv6 over Low power Wireless Personal Area Network (6LoWPAN) enables the resource-constrained, power-constrained and time-constrained IoT devices to communicate over the existing IPv6 network [10]. Thus, the decision of minimal protocol set can be effectively used to manage the IoT devices. A general four-layer protocol stack for IoT devices is shown in Fig. 1.

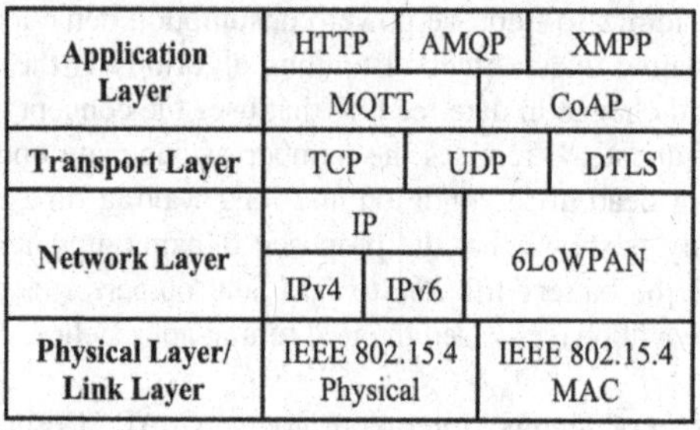

Application Layer	HTTP	AMQP	XMPP
	MQTT		CoAP
Transport Layer	TCP	UDP	DTLS
Network Layer	IP		6LoWPAN
	IPv4	IPv6	
Physical Layer/ Link Layer	IEEE 802.15.4 Physical		IEEE 802.15.4 MAC

Fig. 1. Four layer protocol stack for IoT devices

Selection of a standard internet protocol specially designed for the machine-to-machine communication within the IoT environment is the major concern for researchers. Some common application layer internet protocols accepted for IoT environment are [9]: Hyper Text Transfer Protocol (HTTP), Advance Message Queuing Protocol (AMQP), Extensible Messaging and Presence Protocol (XMPP), Message Queuing Telemetry Transfer (MQTT) Protocol and Constrained Application Proto-col (CoAP).

CoAP is created by Internet Engineering Task Force (IETF) Constrained RESTFUL Environment (CoRE) working group [2, 3, 11]. Its working is similar to HTTP [2, 3] as it follows the REST paradigm and is built on the top of UDP/IP to support congestion control and flow control. It supports 6LoWPAN [3] of IP that can easily manage the transmission of messages to fit into the small header of UDP i.e., into a single frame of IEEE 802.15.4 to minimize the fragmentation. CoAP is a lightweight protocol that is designed especially for the constrained IoT devices. It is client-server based protocol that follows the request-response based communication procedure and uses various HTTP request control packets such as GET, PUT, POST and DELETE; response codes and method codes [8, 11, 12]. In contrary to HTTP, CoAP handles the occurring interchanges asynchronously. This happens over the datagram-oriented transport layer protocol i.e., UDP. Moreover, each CoAP message is shared to the users in the form of tokens and each token has its unique identification number encapsulated with it which helps in detecting message duplication. It does not create full feature set like TCP as many times messages may arrive out of order which witness message duplicity or it may go missing without any notice. CoAP supports simple stop and wait retransmission readability which logically fables the optional reliability. Apart from these, CoAP is optionally bound to combine with Datagram Transport Layer Security (DTLS) protocol of transport layer to provide high level of communications security for IoT systems [11]. CoAP with DTLS gains the benefit of lower overhead and reduced latency for a secure communication in IoT environment.

CoAP supports four types of messages [8, 11]: Confirmable, Non-confirmable, Acknowledgement and Reset. A confirmable CoAP message is reliable and is sent to its destination server again and again until the sender gets an acknowledgement of the message. If the server finds any trouble in managing the request made to it, then it responds to sender with reset message instead of acknowledgement. The non-confirmable is unreliable which don't contain any critical information. Confirmable and non-confirmable messages both go through duplicate deletion procedure. CoAP is considered as the two-tier protocol as it performs its request-response functionality and message transmission in between the application and transport layer. Figure 2 shows a two-tier structure describing the CoAP functionality.

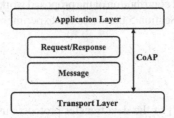

Fig. 2. CoAP functionality

A constrained environment of IoT shows various traits in device-to-device communication such as sleepy nodes, dispersed network and the distributed network where the multicast of the data stream is not efficient [3, 15]. Direct discovery of resources is not practical for the described scenarios and requires an entity namely, Resource Directory (RD) comprises of the information about resources present on other servers (endpoints) that allows lookups for those resources. RD is used as repository of registrations that implements a set of REST interfaces for endpoints to register, manage RD registrations and to lookup resources from RD. The resource discovery is done in five steps: Finding RD, Uniform Resource Identifier (URI) discovery, registration, operations on registration resources, resource lookup [15]. CoAP provides resource discovery mechanism and operates in two different modes i.e., distributed and centralized [2, 3]. In distributed

mode, a sensor node offers a unicast request message to another sensor node to dis-
cover the resources on the behalf of that node, if it is not able to perform the action.
In centralized mode, RD host and maintain the updated service information of every
node within a preconfigured domain correspondingly and respond the service requests
on the behalf of any node [2, 5]. The client requests for the re-sources identified by URI
and RD responses with success and failure. The nodes periodically update the messages
associated with its latest service status to RD to keep it fully updated [6].

CoAP has the characteristic of periodical update and service status of nodes is informed to the RD in every ten seconds of time interval to keep the overall network
up-to-date [4]. However, duplicity of messages arises due to periodical update and battery drainage of node increases due to number of increased updates with decrease in
update interval. The number of duplicate updates increases with the decrease in update
interval that causes increase in power consumption. Though the increase in update interval prolongs the battery lifetime, it may lead to outdated service information [2–5]. This
paper focuses on modification in update interval of standard CoAP as well as the RD
update mechanism together. For this purpose, a novel energy-efficient communication
procedure is designed to increase the network lifetime in IoT environment by reducing
the number of duplicate updates. A dynamic interval tuning algorithm has been proposed
that updates the Resource Directory (RD) with data reading by attenuating the standard
time interval and battery level of IoT devices. The interval tuning approach uses data
reading and battery slot as the parameters. Odd and even concept of message update has
been evaluated where the odd update does not support duplicate updates while the even
does. It has been analyzed a drastic increase in battery lifetime on odd update for each
battery interval.

The rest of the paper is organized as such: Sect. 2 provides literature review; Sect. 3
describes the motivation and contribution of the proposed work; Sect. 4 puts up the details
of proposed methodology. Section 5 discusses the experiments and result analysis; and
Sect. 6 concludes the paper.

2   Literature Review

A comparative analysis [12] of the data transfer protocols used for IoT system shows
CoAP as the most suitable protocol for IoT devices in terms of message size, overhead,
power consumption behaviour, resource requirement, bandwidth and latency. In [11, 12],
the authors have analyzed various protocols and presented CoAP as the most suitable web
transfer protocol for use with constrained IoT devices as it follows Representational State
Transfer (REST) paradigm that facilitates the scalability of network, uniform interfaces
and development of architectural components.

A research study [14] inspects some state-of-art techniques for energy saving in
CoAP based IoT environment. It demonstrates a comparative analysis of studies describing the energy saving techniques based on various parameters such as power saving, data
pressure and security mechanism.

In [2], the authors have analyzed the need of periodic adjustment of update messages
instead of regular updates as it results in extra signaling overhead and high battery
drainage. It required to tune the time interval for information update and an adaptive
tuning approach in between the CoAP clients and CoAP-RD has been proposed. The

proposed approach adjusts the update interval by deciding the battery level of nodes. It also shows its outperformance than standard CoAP when the number of hops in between the node and CoAP-RD server is around 3–4.

An adaptive fibonacci function based time interval tuning algorithm [3] has been proposed in which the counter-based Fibonacci function assigns multiplying factor to standard time interval in contrary to the fixed multiplication value. The Fibonacci based interval tuning gains better results than crisp multiplying factors.

An application-based power saving approach [4] uses the idea of change in recorded data to update the resource directory (RD). The update is performed to the existing RD only when the current observed data is different from the previous data recorded. A threshold time limit of 300 s is configured to avoid the dead node situation. This means the RD will be updated after 300 s, even when no difference in current and antecedent data is observable. Another advantage of this approach is no requirement of modification in standard time interval.

In [13], the authors have presented a design model that focuses on sleepy node condition for scheduling which is considered as an obstacle in direct discovery of nodes. CoAP based communication network allows the clients to search a CoAP node from the RD which has already registered its status to RD and then the client can access that node. The proposed approach elaborates the concept of middleware which consists of RD and Message Queue (MQ) broker for publish-subscribe functionality. A CoAP node goes to its sleep state once it publishes the data to MQ broker.

3 Motivation and Contribution

The state-of-the-art studies reveal that CoAP is the best suitable and reliable protocol for constrained IoT devices which is used to improve power consumption behavior, decrease resource requirements, lower the bandwidth usages and reduce latency. CoAP incurs the lowest message size and overhead too as it uses UDP which works on fire and forget basis. It does not need to spend time in establishing connection and releasing it unlike TCP. It results in no connection overhead. Moreover, the fragmentation of packets into descendant layer results in the depleted packet delivery probability in the network. This also increases the message overhead. CoAP reduces the number of fragmentation and keeps message overhead small. Although, CoAP shows better results than other inter-net protocols, it arises an issue of duplicate message updates. Constrained application protocol has a standard time interval of 10 s for the update. Thus, RD gets updated in every 10 s. The energy is consumed unnecessarily in updating even when no difference in antecedent and present data is recorded. This situation is a boon for duplicate updates. It urge for a power saving approach that updates the data only when a change in present data is recorded. However, It may arise dead node condition and long waiting time of RD.

Some techniques [2, 3] has been proposed to deal with the mentioned issues using the dynamic power tuning and standard time interval tuning concept with the aim to improve power consumption, packet delivery ratio, reduce transmission time, improve network lifetime and security of data. An energy saving technique [4] considers the change recorded instead of standard time interval tuning to update the RD and avoids the dead node situation by updating the similar data in every five minutes when no change has been recorded. Although, it consumes less energy than the existing research works, it does not consider the status of node and results in long waiting time of RD condition as well as high number of message updates. Reduction in duplicate update of messages is still untouched area. This has motivated us to propose a method that aims to reduce the number of duplicate updates and avoid the dead node condition as well as long waiting time of RD condition. The novel contributions behind the design of energy-efficient communication procedure using CoAP for IoT devices are listed as below:

1. To provide a technique of alternate update based on the recorded change in data reading to reduce the number of duplicate updates and improve power consumption behaviour.
2. To keep RD up-to-date by sending the data reading to it with current battery status and previous update status. It helps in avoiding the issue of dead node condition and thus, long waiting time of RD.
3. Dynamic tuning of update interval based on the battery level status to improve the node lifetime.

4   Proposed Methodology

The proposed methodology elaborates a hybrid form of dynamic interval tuning and the update of data reading to RD based on odd and even concept. It has been assumed that each node discovers RD by state configuration or by making announcement. This technique keeps an eye on synchronizing the message update frequency in accordance with the current battery level available for use. It builds a relationship between time interval, battery status and the value of present and antecedent data for the purpose. The standard time interval of CoAP server has been tuned for the update in accordance with battery percentage slot and data reading received. Algorithm 1 describes a dynamic update interval tuning algorithm, which considers the "odd/even update" function based on the threshold value of percentage battery level (BL) used for the update interval tuning. The assumption of threshold value expressed for percentage battery level of node has been taken as 70%, 50%, 25%, and 5% for the update interval tuning. A binary coding is considered to send the node battery status: 11 coded for battery level more than 70% and less than 100%; 10 for more than 50% and less than 70%; 01 for more than 25% and less than 50%, 00 for more than 5% and less than 25%. This will be sent as extended message to RD, which attenuates the update interval by matching the node's battery level. Various cases for update interval tuning have been defined as below.

Case 1: BL $>=$ 70% - The standard time interval of CoAP for updating the RD has been tuned 3 times i.e., 30 s.

Case 2: BL $>=$ 50% - The standard time interval of CoAP for updating the RD has been tuned 3.5 times i.e., 35 s.

Case 3: BL $>=$ 25% - The standard time interval of CoAP for updating the RD has been tuned 4 times i.e., 40 s.

Case 4: BL $>=$ 5% - The standard time interval of CoAP for updating the RD has been tuned 4.5 times i.e., 45 s.

Case 5: BL > 0% - Emergency call is alerted and node dead is notified.

Algorithm 1: Dynamic Update Interval Tuning Algorithm

BL: Battery Level
RD: Resource Directory
//
Begin
Set BL=100%
For (i=1, 2,3.........n)
  Send the data reading with preceding update status and current BL to RD.
    If (BL ≥ 70%), Then
      {
         Wait 3   (Standard time interval)
         Update RD with data reading by toggling between odd and even update
      }
    Else
      If (70% > BL ≥ 50%), Then
        {
           Wait 3.5   (Standard time interval)
           Update RD with data reading by toggling between odd and even update.
        }
    Else
      If (50% > BL ≥ 25%), Then
        {
           Wait 4× (Standard time interval)
           Update RD with data reading by toggling between odd and even update.
        }
    Else
      If (25% > BL ≥ 5%), Then
        {
           Wait 4.5   (Standard time interval)
           Update RD with data reading by toggling between odd and even update.
        }
    Else
      If (BL < 5%), Then
        {
             Emergency Call and broadcast sending node as dead node.
        }
    Calculate the residual power of the sending node: $P_{residual} = P_{initial} - \Delta P$
    Set BL = $P_{residual}$
End For
//

The update of data reading has been done with an alternate odd and even type of update together in different time intervals. Odd message update demonstrates that the CoAP-RD server will not be updated if there is no change found in the data reading under the defined update interval. However, even update force the node to update the RD even if there is no change in the collected data with the awareness of node battery status (dead or active). The battery status added with the present and preceding data are sent as a descriptive message to RD from the node. In every case, RD observes the preceding update status (odd or even update), current battery condition (dead or active) and accordingly updates the present data reading in assigned time interval with the counter update of preceding one. For this purpose, RD assigns an appropriate battery slot for each data reading based on node battery status and the data is updated in the defined time interval of that battery slot. The data reading is updated to RD with the odd update firstly and then with even update into same time interval and the process alternatively continues till the expiration of that battery slot. Same servicing method is followed for all the categorized battery slots. Figure 3 shows the flow diagram of the proposed methodology.

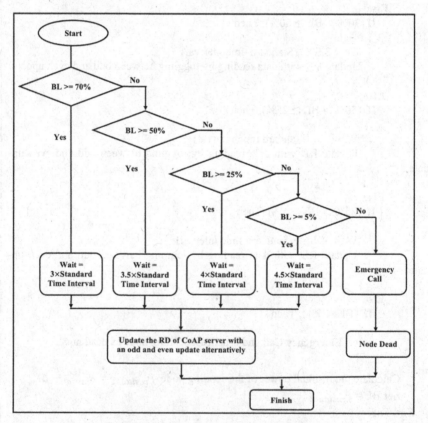

Fig. 3. Flow diagram of proposed methodology

The odd and even concept of update reduces the number of duplicate updates. Although, using the odd update only is more effective in reducing the duplicate updates, it results in dead node condition and long waiting time of RD. Dead node condition arises where the node which is going to be dead has already sent the data reading to RD and the data reading will be sent again and again to RD for the update even after being the node dead. Another condition having long waiting time of RD for update may be raised when there is no update recorded by RD because of either the RD is finding the similar data reading or the node has gone to dead condition without informing the RD. To avoid the situation, the odd and even update together alternatively is used. It helps the server to keep RD up-to-date even if no change in data is recorded by reducing the long waiting time to a maximum of 60 s for battery level greater than 70%, 70 s for battery level in between 50% to 70%, 80 s for battery level in between 25% to 50% and 90 s for battery level in between 5% to 25%. Thus, mitigating the issue of dead node condition at the same time. The information updated about the battery status also helps in resolving the issue of long waiting time and dead node condition as the RD knows about the dead nodes. It leads to a drastic improve in power consumption resulting increased battery lifetime. Interval tuning also improves the network lifetime as it increases with the increase in update interval. Nevertheless, increase in update interval leads to outdated service update, an improved overall network lifetime is achieved.

5 Experiments and Analysis

The performance of proposed method has been evaluated in terms of residual power and node lifetime. The residual battery of node ($P_{residual}$) is calculated by measuring the initial battery level ($P_{initial}$) associated with the data reading and the power consumed (ΔP) in updating it to the RD. The residual battery of node can be calculated using Eq. 1.

$$P_{residual} = P_{initial} - \Delta P \tag{1}$$

The total power consumption (ΔP_{Total}) in updating n number of data readings in a time interval t can be calculated using Eq. 2.

$$\Delta P_{Total}(t) = \sum_{i=1}^{n} \Delta P \tag{2}$$

The percentage residual energy in time interval t' can be calculated using Eq. 3.

$$P_{residual}(t') = \frac{P_{initial} - \Delta P_{Total}(t')}{P_{initial}} \times 100 \tag{3}$$

A node lifetime has been computed as time taken from the start of message sent to RD until the battery level reaches to 5% as it is the lowest battery level considered for performance. Thus, the total network lifetime can be defined as the total time taken in becoming all the nodes dead.

Node.js run-time environment has been used to develop server side and networking applications. Node.js is a lightweight and efficient event-driven and non-blocking I/O model for real-time applications. Visual Studio code editor has been used together with Node.js run-time environment for the implementation. The dataset [7] has been collected from 54 sensors deployed in Intel Berkley research lab. It contains a log of about 2.3 million readings having timestamped topology information along with temperature, humidity, and light intensity. The battery used in the sensor devices is Lithium-ion cells that maintain a fairly constant voltage over their lifetime. A fully charged battery has been considered of 7000 mJ (i.e., 100%) at the deployment stage. The experimental settings details are incorporated in Table 1.

Table 1. Experimental configuration details

Parameters	Values
Node type	TMote Sky
Routing protocol	RPL
Radio environment	Unit Disk Graph Medium (UDGM)
Number of nodes	1–54
Simulation duration	Variable
Full battery	7000 mJ
Transmission range	50 m
Standard update interval	10 s

The result analysis shows that the proposed dynamic update interval tuning method which uses the concept of alternate odd and even update outperforms the primitive models of dynamic power tuning [2] and adaptive fibonacci-based tuning [3] technique in terms of power consumption behavior. A single node power consumption behavior with decrease in battery level in different time intervals has been taken into consideration for the result analysis. However, the variation in result can be found with the number of node count. Figure 4 shows a comparative analysis of power consumption behavior of different tuning approaches. The proposed dynamic update interval tuning approach extends the node lifetime to 70%. The battery lifetime extended is 28% more than without tuning method, 21% more than the dynamic power tuning method [2] and 16% more than adaptive fibonacci-based tuning method [3].

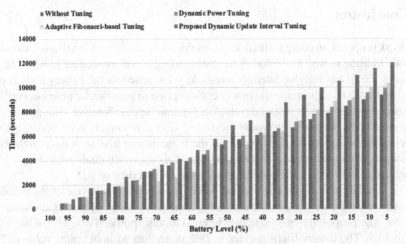

Fig. 4. Comparative analysis of power consumption behavior

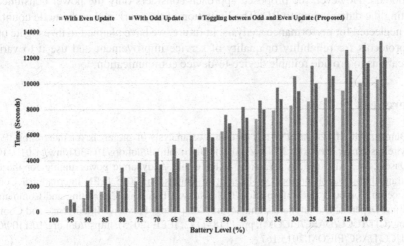

Fig. 5. Power consumption behavior analysis for different types of updates

Figure 5 depicts that odd update procedure shows better power consumption behavior than dynamic update interval tuning and even update procedure. The comparative analysis determines that odd update performs 11% better than proposed dynamic update interval and 29% better than the even update when it comes to reducing duplicate updates. Nevertheless, odd update procedure fails to solve the dead node condition and long waiting time of RD condition. Even update considers the duplicate updates as well as both the issues of odd update procedure included with it. The overall best result is being achieved with the dynamic update interval tuning which consider the toggling of update in between the odd and even.

6   Conclusion

This work proposes an energy-efficient communication model for CoAP in IoT to extend
the node lifetime as well as to modify the data reading update procedure to RD. The aim
is to keep the RD as fully updated. A threshold value based on the battery level is used
to update the RD to determine the power consumption in a particular time interval. The
proposed communication model develops a dynamic update interval tuning algorithm
that considers the odd and even type of message update alternatively in the update interval
of every defined battery level. It maintains the frequency of update of data on the basis
of residual power and change in data readings. This approach deals with the issues of
duplicate updates, dead node condition and long waiting time of RD.

The simulation results show that the power consumption behavior of the proposed
approach outperforms the primitive existing models in terms of power consumption
behavior. The proposed dynamic update interval tuning approach extends the node lifetime to 70%. The battery lifetime extends 28% more than without tuning method, 21%
more than the dynamic power tuning and 16% more than adaptive fibonacci-based tuning method. However, the proposed approach considers only the power consumed in
updating the data reading to RD. The limitation of the work is that the node count has
been neglected for performance analysis. In future, we have planned to investigate other
IoT protocols for reliability or quality of service improvement and use it to various
applications to provide reliable device-to-device communication.

References

1. Qumber Ali, H., Ghani, D.S.: A comparative analysis of protocols for integrating IP and
   wireless sensor networks. J. Netw. **11**(01) (2016). https://doi.org/10.4304/jnw.11.01.1-10
2. Qasem, M., Al-Dubai, A., Yassien, M.B., et al.: A dynamic power tuning for the constrained application protocol of Internet of Things. In: 2015 IEEE International Conference on Computer and Information Technology; Ubiquitous Computing and Communications; Dependable, Autonomic and Secure Computing; Pervasive Intelligence and Computing (CIT/IUCC/DASC/PICOM), pp. 1118–1122. IEEE (2015). https://doi.org/10.1109/CIT/
   IUCC/DASC/PICOM.2015.167
3. Albalas, F., Mardini, W., Al-Soud, M.: AFT: adaptive Fibonacci-based tuning protocol for
   service and resource discovery in the Internet of Things. In: 2017 Second International Conference on Fog and Mobile Edge Computing (FMEC), pp. 177–182 (2017). https://doi.org/
   10.1109/FMEC.2017.7946427
4. Mardini, W., Yassein, M.B., AlRashdan, M., Alsmadi, A., Amer, A.B.: Application-based
   power saving approach for IoT CoAP protocol. In: E-learning and Information Systems 2018
   (DATA 2018), Madrid, Spain, 1–2 October 2018, 5 pages. ACM, New York (2018). https://
   doi.org/10.1145/3279996.3280008
5. Yassein, M.B., et al.: Challenges and techniques of constrained application protocol (CoAP)
   for efficient energy consumption. In: 2020 11th International Conference on Information and
   Communication Systems (ICICS) (2020). https://doi.org/10.1109/icics49469.2020.239564
6. Yasin, M.B., Abuein, Q., Amer, A.B., Qasem, M.: An energy-efficient technique for constrained application protocol of Internet of Things. In: 2016 International Conference on
   Engineering and MIS (ICEMIS) (2016). https://doi.org/10.1109/icemis.2016.7745305
7. https://www.kaggle.com/divyansh22/intel-berkeley-research-lab-sensor-data

8. Colitti, W., Steenhaut, K., De Caro, N., Buta, B., Dobrota, V.: Evaluation of constrained application protocol for wireless sensor networks. In: 18th IEEE Workshop on LANMAN, pp. 1–6 (2011)
9. Al-Fuqaha, A., Guizani, M., Mohammadi, M., Aledhari, M., Ayyash, M.: Internet of Things: a survey on enabling technologies, protocols, and applications. IEEE Commun. Surv. Tutor. 17(4), 2347–2376 (2015). https://doi.org/10.1109/COMST.2015.2444095
10. Sehgal, A., Perelman, V., Kuryla, S., Schonwalder, J.: Management of resource constrained devices in the Internet of Things. IEEE Commun. Mag. 50(12), 144–149 (2012). https://doi.org/10.1109/mcom.2012.6384464
11. Iglesias-Urkia, M., Orive, A., Urbieta, A.: Analysis of CoAP implementations for Industrial Internet of Things: a survey. Procedia Comput. Sci. 109, 188–195 (2017). https://doi.org/10.1016/j.procs.2017.05.323. ISSN 1877-0509
12. Naik, N.: Choice of effective messaging protocols for IoT systems: MQTT, CoAP, AMQP and HTTP. In: 2017 IEEE International Systems Engineering Symposium (ISSE) (2017). https://doi.org/10.1109/syseng.2017.8088251
13. Jin, W., Kim, D.H.: A sleep-awake scheme based on CoAP for energy-efficiency in Internet of Things. Int. J. Inform. Visual. 1(4) (2017). ISSN 2549-9610
14. Yassein, M.B., Hmeidi, I., Alghazo, F., Odat, B., Smairat, A.: Energy saving techniques in CoAP of Internet of Things. In: DATA 2021: International Conference on Data Science, E-learning and Information Systems 2021, Ma'an, Jordan. 5–7 April 2021, pp. 124–130 (2021). https://doi.org/10.1145/3460620.3460743
15. Wang, Y., Wei, G.: An implementation of CoAP-based resource directory in Californium. In: BDIOT 2018: Proceedings of the 2018 2nd International Conference on Big Data and Internet of Things, October 2018, pp. 148–152 (2018). https://doi.org/10.1145/3289430.3289439

A Systematic Study on LoRa Communication in IoT: Implementation Challenges and Research Solutions

Rishi Mistry⬡, Marcelo Neves(✉)⬡, and Bhargavi Goswami(✉)⬡

School of Computer Science, Queensland University of Technology, Brisbane, QLD 4000,
Australia
rishinitin.mistry@connect.qut.edu.au, m.neves@hdr.qut.edu.au,
goswamib@qut.edu.au

Abstract. LoRa (Long Range) technology is one of those Internet of Things (IoT) technologies aimed to develop a name in the IoT industry for affordable yet efficient applications. This technology explicitly provides a comprehensive wireless solution for communication between LoRa capable devices for long-range, low-power, and efficient use. Researchers have provided empirical evidence of the use of LoRa devices in IoT applications for the industry. To our knowledge, hardly information is available on configuring the LoRa enabled End-nodes using the STM32 with the SX1280 device. With Semtech devices, this research will focus on the detailed study of applications of Semtech SX1280 devices and their functionalities to set up a single gateway and multiple End-nodes. Documentation such as the product datasheets, user manuals, online information, and the detailed performance reports from Semtech and STM are considered participants of data collection to analyze the data collected and present it in a meaningful manner in the form of a user guide. Online sources from Semtech have been a significant lead to identifying the functionalities of the SX1280 devices. The purpose of this chapter is to provide at a single point of concentration a large amount of verified and certified information into preparing the LoRa Gateway for efficient communication with multiple End-nodes. The collected information has proved useful for effectively setting up and configuring the Gateway in a detailed step-by-step guide. Additionally, the Gateway functions are also explored in detail for one-way communication. The in-depth analysis indicates the possibility for the practical use of SX1280 devices in IoT applications. However, the devices need to be compatible with the environment, such as performance affecting parameters and other possible topological scenarios covered in this research.

Keywords: LoRa communication · STM simulator · Semtech devices · IoT · Wireless gateway · Sensors · Long-range sensors network

1 Introduction

There is a tremendous development in Internet of Things (IoT) technology in recent years. One of the popular communication technologies for IoT is LoRa (Long Range).

It is a wireless technology used to transmit data over long distances. Typically, at a lower data rate (few kbps), this technology can be helpful in applications where the range is a primary factor and power to transmit and sense. There are demonstrations with empirical evidence on the uses of LoRa in IoT using different variants of devices and vendors; however, implementation of the LoRa devices and specifically configuring the SX1280 series is not known and pictured anywhere in a direct fashion. Thus, the need for a complete user guide on setting up and using SX1280 devices was imminent. This research aims to fill in this research gap, which can answer the functions of the Semtech SX1280 devices, which are used to set up and manage the connections between a single gateway and multiple end nodes tested in the real world. There is no previous research or detailed literature that focuses on setting up and configuring these devices. Nevertheless, some researchers have used these Semtech series devices to demonstrate performance evaluations and test LoRa technology limits.

Recent research has occurred to test the network performance characteristics and measurements and develop sufficient models for using LoRa in a simulation model. Proposal [2] discussed the performance evaluations of LoRa technology inside campus building environments and how the connection was affected based on parameters such as walls, ceilings, and other obstructions. Proposals [3] and [4] focused on the network performance parameter of scalability, which was the primary factor of their approach. Further, they demonstrate adding a more significant number of end nodes per Gateway in simulations and experiments, respectively. However, these findings did not illustrate the configuration of the gateway and end nodes in the IoT scenario. The integration of LoRa in an IoT setting is in particular challenging due to the various limitations and policy enforcements of the IoT setting. At the same time, security is an important factor.

To the best of our knowledge, no research or online resource clearly explain or present a guide to enable a user to use the SX1280 Gateway, utilize its functionalities and connect to end node together for uplink and downlink communication. Thus, this motivates us to do literature analysis and additional methods to analyze resource materials relevant to this research question. A thorough literature analysis is a way to achieve the expected outcomes. The literature analysis on the user guides, reference manuals of the SX1280 device kits, and detailed explanations provided in datasheets are the critical online resource materials for the study. The outcomes of this research provide a brief user guide illustrating step-by-step processes with details on the necessary functionalities of the LoRa devices and kits [1]. The tangible outcome is a "How-to" guide. To produce even more tangible outcomes, one would have to physically apply the gained knowledge to use the features and functionalities according to the guidelines. The results indicate completed research that can be used as a reference guide to give the reader a head start on using Semtech SX1280 device functions and setting up and configuring the communication between a gateway and end node devices efficiently. This literature has also shown the one-way communication between the gateway and end node.

Section 2 surveys the literature on LoRa and the different methods taken by other researchers to test the LoRa technology. Section 3 outlines the methodologies and techniques which take place to collect and analyse the relevant data which is used in this research. Section 4 determine and analyse the data collected. Section 5 includes the findings and results after analysing the relevant data collected.

2 Related Work

A range of research on LoRa devices has focused on the details of tests on capabilities of LoRa technology, and the proven results have shown evidence on their performance parameters. In [2], experiments were conducted experiments using the Semtech SX1278 series device and AQD (Air Quality Detector) as nodes to measure the effect on the communication link from external obstructions such as in a campus environment. In newer research, [3] found a method to test LoRa technology in network performance based on the combination of a simulation method and experiments. Similarly, the scalability of the network was tested on the simulation model by comparing different interference measurements [4]. Also, [7] have conducted tests in a deployed UAV-enabled network for applications in disaster management, indicating the performance of LoRaWAN. Moreover, only a few research studies have used the SX1280 devices, such as [5] and [6].

A Large set of researchers have implemented IoT networks as the last mile technology managed by software-defined networks for comparing the performance of controllers [8, 9]. A similar situation is observed when applications like vehicular networks [10] smart grids [11] and congested corporate networks [12] are implemented. Handoff [13, 14] and scalability [15, 16] are also studied with IoT as physical infrastructure and SDN implemented at higher layers [17, 18]. LoRa implementation on simulation is studied using SDN controllers of Ryu [19], Beacon [20], Onos [21], OpenMul [22], FloodLight [23], Pyrectic and Franetic [24]. Further, load balancing [25] and security [26, 27] are also explored in the simulation environment for LoRa.

However, these researchers do not indicate how to configure the Gateway and the End-node conveniently. This research explains the question of a) how to use SX1280 LoRa devices, b) how to program them and use their functions relevant to the applications. This new knowledge would have paved the way for novel research relevant to other variants of LoRa devices. Hence, this research motivates us to answer the questions on how to program, set up, and use the utilities of these Semtech devices with a Gateway and End-nodes setup.

3 Methodology

A systematic literature analysis procedure was followed as part of the literature survey, which required selecting data sources that would prove helpful information to pursue this data-driven approach. After carefully selecting participants for data collection, it was necessary to extract meaningful data from the collected data relevant to the research question.

3.1 Process

After the literature analysis on LoRa was done, it was necessary to develop a criterion list for the literature that would strictly focus on answering the research question in this chapter. The criterion included terms related to LoRa Gateway, End-node, how to program, how to set up, how to establish a communication link and use the SX1280 devices efficiently. This required gathering information specific to SX1280 and the use of its features and utilities. The diagram provided in Fig. 1 represents the research methodology followed to demonstrate the process on what to collect, what data to analyse and finally what to report. This step by step process would require three main tasks to be done. Firstly, collection of specific data from different data sources such as User manuals, Development guides, user posts from the development portals and other important information with the help of internet directing towards critical information about code required to configure and manage LoRa devices. Secondly, analysis of the collected data based on themes. This task required segregating collected data into different themes based on the nature of the data. Data collected would then be helpful to interpret based on themes such as literature, hardware, software and other several themes relevant to LoRa SX1280. Finally, the finding from the analysis would then be required to be reported into a presentable manner such as a user guide or user manual to develop LoRaWan communication using STM devices.

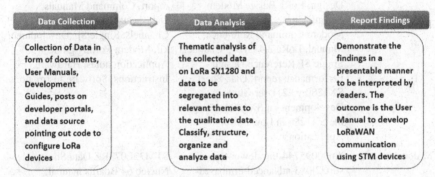

Fig. 1. A step-by-step methodology procedure is divided into three phases, each resulting intangible outcomes.

3.2 Data Collection

It was necessary to identify data sources before any relevant data could be collected for collecting the data. Also, a criterion for collecting needed to be set to only LoRa, LoRaWAN, SX1280 devices, and STM32 related files, documents, and other relevant information sources.

The first step was to establish a thorough foundation and base knowledge about LoRa literature. There was ample literature available through the sources over internet websites. The leadfinalizeding websites considered for this literature analysis included QUT library, IEEE Xplore, Semtech, STM, Mobilefish.com for LoRaWAN, and many other sources such as videos about LoRa technology uses. Additionally, the documents and scholarly articles were also considered by Google Scholars to get around all the information on LoRa technology. A brief list of documents collected from the selected data participants is listed in Table 1.

Table 1. List of data participants, sources, and related thematic information extracted during data collection.

Data sources	Data participants	Thematic information
Websites	MobileFish, Semtech, LoRa l Developer Portal	LoRa literature, Hardware Instructions, SX1280
Article sites	QUT Library, IEEE Xplore, mdpi, Google Scholars, Elsevier	LoRa literature, SX1280, Software Instructions, Simulation, Uplink, Downlink, RSSI, Performance, Evaluation, Network Performance, Communication link, Environment, Scalability, LOS scenarios
Semtech documents	User Guide to the LoRa® 2.4 GHz 3 Channels Single SF Reference Design, LoRa Basics Modem Porting Guide, LoRa Basics Modem Command Reference Manual, LoRa 2.4 GHz 3 Channels Single SF Reference Design - Performance report, Data Sheet SX1280 v3.2, User Guide Development kit SX1280, Using the SX1280 in Low Power Applications	LoRa literature, Reference Design, Design Models, Performance report, Command Manuals, Datasheets, User guide, SX1280, 3 Channels, Single SF, Development kit, Modem Porting guide, Application notes, Hardware Instructions, Software Instructions
STM documents	dm00095744-ultralowpower-stm32l0x3-advanced-armbased-32bit-mcus-stmicroelectronics, dm00105823-stm32-nucleo64-boards-mb1136-stmicroelectronics, dm00105928-getting-started-with-stm32-nucleo-board-software-development-tools-stmicroelectronics, dm00114438-getting-started-with-stm32cubel0-for-stm32l0-series-stmicroelectronics, Data Sheet stm32l073rz	STM32L073RZ Data Sheet, Nucleo 64 Boards manual, Software instructions, Hardware instructions, Tool guide for STM32, Getting started guide with STM32CubeIDE Manual
Videos	YouTube videos	IoT, IoT architecture, LoRa in IoT, LoRaWAN/LoRa, LoRa literature

3.3 Analysis

The next step was to extract meaningful data from the selected data participants to analyse the collected data. The information was needed to be identified into specific themes for the analysis, which required some thematic analysis of the collected data.

After evaluating the data into pieces, the following themes were finalised, which were used to provide the initial foundation for the 'User Guide' result.

Table 2. The information was extracted for each type of theme (criterion).

Themes (criterion)	Data participants used for extracting information
Hardware requirements – SX1280 GW and STM32L073RZ Nucleo	For Gateway - LoRa Basics Modem Porting Guide User Guide Development kit SX1280, Using the SX1280 in Low Power Applications For End Node - Data Sheet stm32l073rz, dm00095744-ultralowpower-stm32l0x3-advanced-armbased-32bit-mcus-stmicroelectronics, dm00114438-getting-started-with-stm32cubel0-for-stm32l0-series-stmicroelectronics
Software requirements - gateway_2g4_hal software from GitHub for GW, STM32 software, lorabasicsmodem-master.zip for End node programming	For Gateway - LoRa Basics Modem Command Reference Manual, User Guide Development kit SX1280, User Guide to the LoRa® 2.4GHz 3 Channels Single SF Reference Design For End Node - dm00095744-ultralowpower-stm32l0x3-advanced-armbased-32bit-mcus-stmicroelectronics, dm00114438-getting-started-with-stm32cubel0-for-stm32l0-series-stmicroelectronics
Reference guides - Setting up Gateway one-way communication design model for SX1280 Gateway	User Guide Development kit SX1280, User Guide to the LoRa® 2.4 GHz 3 Channels Single SF Reference Design

Once the analysis was completed and the data organized in themes, it was essential to refine it to align with the research question. Further, the results needed to be included in a document that could be presented visually and appealable to the document's readers. Hence, the User guide would require each theme separated into different sections to give the information to the reader. Hence, the three main criterions used were set to Software requirements, Hardware requirements, and Reference guides as provided in Table 2.

The Hardware requirements criteria required the collected information to be related to the hardware of the Semtech SX1280 devices specifically. Therefore, for Gateway and End-node, the documents selected would only provide strict hardware instructions for the findings. Additional hardware instructions for products such as Raspberry Pi were also part of these findings.

The Software requirements criteria required only the information for the Gateway device, the software 'gateway_2g4_hal' and the End-nodes, the software' lorabasicsmodem', STM32 Cube IDE. Therefore, the files and readings required to be part of this criteria would be related to the instructions and findings of software, such as installing, setting up, and using the software. Features and functionalities of the mentioned software were also crucial in this research to give the readers a better edge on LoRa technology.

The User guides provided officially on the websites were used to understand specific models and reference designs to make a personal network of LoRa capable devices. Therefore, these reference models had been used to answer the research questions of how-to setup and how to configure the specific SX1280 devices, including the features and configurable settings.

4   Result and Discussion

This section discusses the results and findings of the mentioned methodologies of the previous section.

One of the main goals of this research chapter was to establish a document stating all the essential steps to be undertaken to allow the study of SX1280 devices. Appropriate findings had been obtained using the different themes and aligning them to answer the relevant research questions. The final product of the research is determined to be a User Manual for the SX1280 devices. Manual allows the user to customise with the topological configuration of LoRa technology by following provided programming steps. The question of how to set up the SX1280 devices is answered, using the steps required to set up the Gateway and End-node and allow the devices to be turned on and used as the user wished to.

The User Manual consisted of sections that highlight the essential pieces of information to the reader to allow the user first to understand the structure of the User Manual and the hardware and software requirements. Further, readers can follow step by step guidelines specifically for the Gateway and End-nodes to configure and utilise functionalities of the SX1280 Gateway. The Manual has pointed out the specific functionalities in code, which could be optional for users but valuable for advanced users. Each section in the User Manual has been discussed in detail in the coming subsections.

4.1   Manual Development

This section in the User Manual discusses the intention of the document. It briefly explains the actual contents and what is its use. The noted details were related to hardware, software, and steps to follow in this section. It also informed the reader about any discrepancies the user could or could not face in case of changes or variations from the steps and instructions given in the document. The user was also guided to use the steps as is and not modify any crucial steps as it could change the true nature of the process followed by the user.

4.2 Topology

This User manual section consists of the Network topology that makes the LoRaWAN communication work with the Gateway and End-node links. It also includes the diagram which indicates the mode of communication between the Gateway and End-node, namely uplink and downlink communication. The middle section of Fig. 2 shows the visualization of this section in the manual.

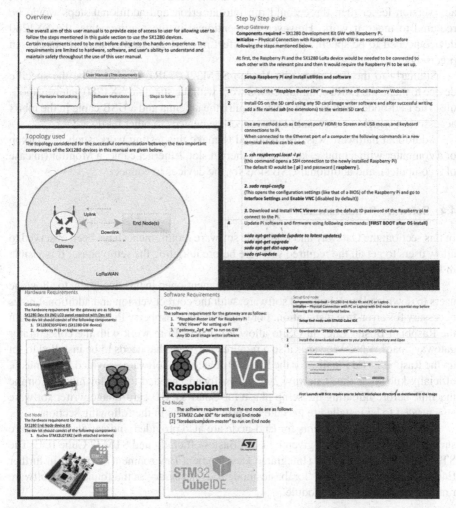

Fig. 2. The Manual visuals: topology description, hardware requirements, software requirements for Gateway, and end-nodes. The figure includes Step by Step guide for setup.

4.3 Hardware Requirements

In this section, the hardware components related to the topology and the design are described in detail and visualized in Fig. 2. The hardware components required are further subdivided into two more sections for Gateway and End-node specifically.

For the Gateway, the devices required are the SX1280Z3DSFGW1 Development Kit and Raspberry Pi, which constitute the Gateway module required for communication. The Raspberry Pi requirements needed to be at least version 3 to operate in this scenario; any version lesser than three could run into an error, and additional steps would be required to make it work. However, as mentioned in the requirements, the SX1280 device needed to be specific as it would affect most of the further steps if not chosen precisely.

Similarly to the End-node, the Nucleo STM32L073RZ needed to be the specific device to make the LoRa communication work with the standard SX1280 gateway module. The End-node module would also require the antenna and a USB cable in the inbox accessories, which were essential to connect the devices to other hardware.

Additional hardware was also required to make this testing work, such as a laptop or a computer with a mouse, keyboard, Ethernet slot, Ethernet cable, a Monitor (in case of a computer), and additional USB slots for the devices to connect.

4.4 Software Requirements

In this section, the Gateway and End-node software requirements have been observed to allow users to get all the required software before initiating the setup phase. It is visible in Fig. 2.

The software requirements for Gateway are mentioned in this document to allow the users to download each required software, with the correct version and additional notes necessary for error-free installation. For Gateway, the Raspberry Pi has to be set up with the Raspbian Buster Lite, an OS to allow Raspberry Pi to work with the concentrator gateway board. VNC Viewer is also a required software that needs to be installed to set up the Raspberry Pi. Finally, for the SX1280 device, the software provided by Semtech, officially known as the 'gateway_2g4_hal' software, needed to be downloaded on the machine before initiating the setup phase for Gateway. SD card image writer software also needed to be installed to execute the provided steps in the following sections.

The software requirements for End-node are also provided, indicating the software such as 'lorabasicsmodem' given by LoRaBasics officially and STM32 Cube IDE. The STM32CubeIDE is an IDE (Integrated Development Environment) required in further End-node setup stages, and 'lorabasicsmodem' is necessary as the foundation software running on the End-node module.

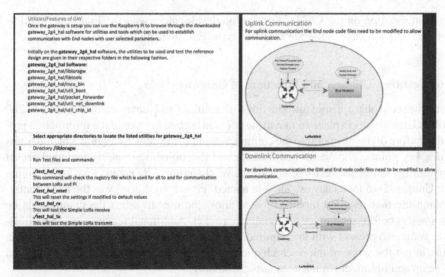

Fig. 3. The manual description includes useful utilities/features and the functionalities available to access the STM features for Gateway. The manual also describes step-by-step procedures to set up uplink and downlink communication.

4.5 Step by Step Guidelines

The summary of the utilities and features, directories, commands to run specific files and the uplink and downlink communication of the gateway can be followed by the user as per their preference after the setting up phase as illustrated in Fig. 3. Figure 3 also illustrates detailed explanation on how to establish uplink and downlink communication with the necessary modifications required to allow the communication to work. The functionalities provided in the gateway software can be used from their respective folders. The detailed functionality of each of the files and the commands to run these files have been summarized in the step-by-step guide mentioned in this section and also been further subdivided into two sections to allow the reader to set up different devices. Please check Fig. 2 and Fig. 3 along with [1]. Therefore, Gateway and End-node connections and set up phases have been divided into further sub-sections.

Set Up a Gateway: Clear instructions before starting the steps are identified and listed as tutorial steps to allow setting the Gateway conveniently. Physical connections with the Raspberry Pi and the SX1280 module were needed to enable users to make all the necessary steps to work mentioned in the document.

Set Up an End-Node: For setting up the End-node, a series of different steps are needed before the End-node becomes ready for gateway communication. Therefore, the End-node physical connections were the initialisation steps done before the setup steps could be performed.

Steps of the entire procedure are given in the User Manual to allow a user to decide any additional settings and directories the user wishes to make. The steps also provide brief information on the C/C++ Application development with the End-node to allow the 'lorabasicsmodem' software to work on the End-node module.

4.6   Features, Utilities, and Functions of Gateway

After the setup phase, a brief introduction to the utilities and functionalities of the SX1280 LoRa Gateway was in place so that the user could take advantage of the information provided before diving deeper into the communication of the devices. Figure 3 includes this phase key points. The mentioned features and functionalities majorly included packet forwarding, testing packet for send and receive, changing LoRa parameters, and changing the Unique ID of the Gateway. The file named 'global_conf.json' was the main configuration file that required modification to allow the user to select the communication parameters before sending or receiving any packet. Additional features and functionalities were also present with the required information regarding software and hardware. Still, as per the scope of the research question, it briefly answered the questions related to setup and uplink/downlink communication only.

4.7   Uplink and Downlink Communication

Uplink Communication: For the Uplink communication to work, modifications and commands were needed to be done separately on the Gateway and the End-node side to make the communication work as expected. The devices must be already set up individually before this step begins as shown in Fig. 3.

The End-node required modifications in the Core and MAC layer files to allow users to send the packets from the End-node device. The device would require a setup with the changes made to successfully send user-defined payload messages as packets on the set LoRa frequency.

On the other hand, the Gateway is set to receive packets and display messages from the relevant End-node with the correct LoRa frequency range set. For receiving packets, configuration steps are to be followed, allowing the Gateway module to receive the packets in the receive slot period with the custom message sent by the user. As encryption was part of this process, the receiver side would also require first decrypting the encrypted message received to recover the original sent message.

Downlink Communication: Like uplink, changes were required on both ends to make the communication possible and recover encrypted messages from Gateway. Different changes were needed on both ends to make the downlink communication work. Modifications on Gateway to send the user-defined messages and pointers in code to identify the payload type, payload format, and payload length on the End-node are listed to allow users to make changes in the coding for customisation of private functions upon receiving a packet. Variables with received payload are provided to enable users to print messages in the terminal to confirm message reception from Gateway.

Although the communication and testing were achieved, there still exists a limitation of making the communication bi-directional altogether. It poses a challenge for future work and should be undertaken as motivation from this chapter's current work.

5 Conclusion and Future Work

This study has attempted to evaluate how will the SX1280 devices be operated clearly and how the user will manage the customized communications. The most significant contribution of this research was the User Manual can be found online at [1], a How-to guide to answer users' questions such as how to configure the Semtech SX1280 Family of devices specifically. All the mentioned communication steps are identified, implemented, and tested beforehand, and multiple attempts have been made to confirm the procedure stated at each stage. This research will benefit IoT Engineers, researchers, and IoT application developers. The outcome of this research will become the base for future IoT Experiments and LoRaWAN functionality enhancements.

Future research may include experimentations of the SX1280 devices based on this guide as a troubleshooting manual. It is expected the next step points out to a high rate of packet collision avoidance in the Gateway/End-node communication, which will allow users to use SX1280 devices for any IoT application of choice suitable with LoRa technology. Other future work can also include testing the limits of LoRa technology in terms of performance evaluations with the methods described in this chapter. In addition, there will be a need for changes in the appropriate configurations both in the Gateway and in the End-nodes, with environmental adaptations to different usage scenarios. There are variations in LOS (line of sight), physical obstructions, fluctuations, density, immunity to other signals in the same frequency range, packet loss, and other parameters that reflect the communication signals between the Gateway and the end-nodes.

Acknowledgment. The authors would like to acknowledge Prof. Yu-Chu Tian, Prof. Yanming Feng, and Prof. Raja Jurdak. They have guided this topic of LoRa to allow working on the User Manual, reflecting the final findings of this research.

References

1. Mistry, R., Goswami, B., Neves, M.: LoRa Experiment step-by-step configuration manual. Research Group of Bhargavi Goswami, 30 November 2021. https://bhg2.files.wordpress.com/2022/01/user-manual-for-sx1280-setup.pdf. Accessed 7 Jan 2022
2. Liang, R., Zhao, L., Wang, P.: Performance evaluations of LoRa wireless communication in building environments. Sensors **20**(14), 3828 (2020)
3. El-Aasser, M., Edward, P., Mandour, M., Ashour, M., Elshabrawy, T.: A comprehensive hybrid bit-level and packet-level LoRa-LPWAN simulation model. Internet Things **14**, 100386 (2021)
4. Haxhibeqiri, J., Van den Abeele, F., Moerman, I., Hoebeke, J.: LoRa scalability: a simulation model based on interference measurements. Sensors **17**(6), 1193 (2017)
5. Zhang, Z., Cao, S., Wang, Y.: A long-range 2.4 G network system and scheduling scheme for aquatic environmental monitoring. Electronics **8**(8), 909 (2019)
6. Andersen, F.R., Ballal, K.D., Petersen, M.N., Ruepp, S.: Ranging capabilities of LoRa 2.4 GHz. In: 2020 IEEE 6th World Forum on Internet of Things (WF-IoT), pp. 1–5. IEEE, June 2020
7. Saraereh, O.A., Alsaraira, A., Khan, I., Uthansakul, P.: Performance evaluation of UAV-enabled LoRa networks for disaster management applications. Sensors **20**(8), 2396 (2020)

8. Shirvar, A., Goswami, B.: Performance comparison of software-defined network controllers. In: 2021 International Conference on Advances in Electrical, Computing, Communication and Sustainable Technologies (ICAECT), pp. 1–13. IEEE, February 2021

9. Lunagariya, D., Goswami, B.: A comparative performance analysis of stellar SDN controllers using emulators. In: 2021 International Conference on Advances in Electrical, Computing, Communication and Sustainable Technologies (ICAECT), pp. 1–9. IEEE, February 2021

10. Goswami, B., Asadollahi, S.: Novel approach to improvise congestion control over vehicular ad hoc networks (VANET). In: 2016 3rd International Conference on Computing for Sustainable Global Development (INDIACom), pp. 3567–3571. IEEE, March 2016

11. Thakre, K., Goswami, B.: Designing neighborhood area networks of smart grid using software defined networks. In: 2021 Fourth International Conference on Electrical, Computer and Communication Technologies (ICECCT), pp. 1–6. IEEE, September 2021

12. Goswami, B., Asadollahi, S., Asare, I.: Performance evaluation of widely implemented congestion control algorithms over diversified networking situations. In: ICCSNIT 2016, Pattaya, Thailand. Open Access (2016)

13. Thomas, L., Sandeep, J., Goswami, B., Paulose, J.: A survey on various handoff methods in mobile ad hoc network environment. In: Elçi, A., Sa, P.K., Modi, C.N., Olague, G., Sahoo, M.N., Bakshi, S. (eds.) Smart Computing Paradigms: New Progresses and Challenges. AISC, vol. 767, pp. 27–60. Springer, Singapore (2020). https://doi.org/10.1007/978-981-13-9680-9_3

14. Thomas, L., Sandeep, J., Goswami, B., Paulose, J.: Handoff schemes in mobile environments: a comparative study. Int. J. Serv. Sci. Manag. Eng. Technol. (IJSSMET) 11(1), 55–72 (2020)

15. Asadollahi, S., Goswami, B., Raoufy, A.S., Domingos, H.G.J.: Scalability of software-defined network on floodlight controller using OFNet. In: 2017 International Conference on Electrical, Electronics, Communication, Computer, and Optimization Techniques (ICEECCOT), pp. 1–5. IEEE, December 2017

16. Asadollahi, S., Goswami, B.: Experimenting with scalability of floodlight controller in software-defined networks. In: 2017 International Conference on Electrical, Electronics, Communication, Computer, and Optimization Techniques (ICEECCOT), pp. 288–292. IEEE, December 2017

17. Kumar, A., Goswami, B., Augustine, P.: Experimenting with resilience and scalability of wifi mininet on small to large SDN networks. Int. J. Recent Technol. Eng. 7(6S5), 201–207 (2019)

18. Goswami, B., Asadollahi, S.S.: Enhancement of LAN infrastructure performance for data center in presence of network security. In: Lobiyal, D.K., Mansotra, V., Singh, U. (eds.) Next-Generation Networks. AISC, vol. 638, pp. 419–432. Springer, Singapore (2018). https://doi.org/10.1007/978-981-10-6005-2_44

19. Asadollahi, S., Goswami, B., Sameer, M.: Ryu controller's scalability experiment on software defined networks. In: 2018 IEEE International Conference on Current Trends in Advanced Computing (ICCTAC), pp. 1–5. IEEE, February 2018

20. Manuel, T., Goswami, B.H.: Experimenting with scalability of beacon controller in software-defined network. Int. J. Recent Technol. Eng. 7(5S2), 550–555 (2019)

21. Sameer, M., Goswami, B.: Experimenting with ONOS scalability on software-defined network. J. Adv. Res. Dyn. Control Syst. 10(14-Special Issue), 1820–1830 (2018)

22. Singh, S., Goswami, B., Paulose, J., Thomas, L.: Implementing and experimenting with Open-MUL scalability in software defined network. J. Netw. Commun. Emerg. Technol. (JNCET), 11(1) (2021)

23. Khan, M.A., Goswami, B., Paulose, J., Thomas, L.: Novel model to inculcate proactive behaviour in programmable switches for floodlight controlled software defined network. Trans. Jpn. Soc. Comput. Eng. Sci. 17(12) (2021)

24. Kulkarni, M., Goswami, B., Paulose, J.: Experimenting with scalability of software defined networks using Pyretic and Frenetic. In: Chaubey, N., Parikh, S., Amin, K. (eds.) COMS2 2021. CCIS, vol. 1416, pp. 168–192. Springer, Cham (2021). https://doi.org/10.1007/978-3-030-76776-1_12
25. Khan, M.A., Goswami, B., Asadollahi, S.: Data visualization of software-defined networks during load balancing experiment using floodlight controller. In: Anouncia, S., Gohel, H., Vairamuthu, S. (eds.) Data Visualization, pp. 161–179. Springer, Singapore (2020). https://doi.org/10.1007/978-981-15-2282-6_9
26. Goswami, B., Wilson, S., Asadollahi, S., Manuel, T.: Data visualization: experiment to impose DDoS attack and its recovery on software-defined networks. In: Anouncia, S., Gohel, H., Vairamuthu, S. (eds.) Data Visualization, pp. 141–160. Springer, Singapore (2020). https://doi.org/10.1007/978-981-15-2282-6_8
27. Bhavsar, V., Sahrial, C., Goswami, B.: Security and performance evaluation of software defined network controllers against distributed denial of service attack. In: 2021 Fourth International Conference on Electrical, Computer and Communication Technologies (ICECCT), pp. 1–8. IEEE, September 2021

A Low Complexity CFO Reduction Technique for LFDMA Systems

Lekshmi R. Nair[1]([✉]) [iD] and Sakuntala S. Pillai[2] [iD]

[1] Sree Narayana Institute of Technology, Adoor, Kerala 691554, India
lekshmiunnikrishnan@gmail.com
[2] Mar Baselios College of Engineering and Technology, Thiruvananthapuram, Kerala 695 015, India

Abstract. Localized Single Carrier Frequency Division Multiple Access (LFDMA) has become a choice of broadband system data transmission of uplink channels, since it has a lower Peak Average Power Ratio (PAPR) compared to multicarrier modulation systems. In LFDMA, the frequency domain equalizers suffer greatly from the Bit Error Rate (BER) performance degradation due to multipath channel impairments such as inter symbol interference (ISI) and carrier frequency offset (CFO), which mainly affect the orthogonality among the subcarriers. In general, CFO degrades the system performance of LFDMA. In this paper, the ISI cancellation approach is employed for the transmission of modulated signals in a fixed wireless environment by combining the banded matrix approximation method with a unique equalization mechanism. Nonlinear equalization based on the modified Volterra (MV) series combines a decision feedback filter with a Volterra equalizer in the back to adapt the distorted signal and reduce multipath impairment. The simulation results show that the proposed method has better BER performance than the other techniques reported so far.

Keywords: BER · CFO · ISI · LFDMA · PAPR

1 Introduction

Increasing demand for wireless communication systems with high data rate and low PAPR values has boosted the significance of single carrier transmission method, called the SC-FDMA system [1]. The low PAPR property of SC-FDMA signals compared to OFDMA, enables the mobile terminal to achieve high data rate with reliable transmission [2]. The SC-FDMA is mainly based on the subcarriers mapping technique, which is categorized into two types, namely Localized SC-FDMA (LFDMA) and Interleaved SCFDMA (IFDMA) [3]. This paper concentrates on LFDMA systems since they are highly sensitive to Carrier Frequency Offset (CFO) compared to IFDMA systems.

LFDMA offers inter symbol interference (ISI) free signal transmission and reduce the equalization complexity by providing nonlinear equalization [4]. ISI is an unwanted noise signal which has a negative impact caused by nearby symbols in the dispersive channel. The nonlinear equalization is an effective solution to eliminate ISI. The aim of this work is to propose a modified Volterra equalization suitable for LFDMA and to demonstrate the effectiveness of the proposed equalizer and to eliminate the ISI induced by the channel. The performance gain is obtained by the cancellation of the multipath impairment at the receiver. An iterative decision feedback equalizer is utilized to eliminate ISI in reference [5]. In reference [6], the author has demonstrated a reduction in the BER performance and also noise cancellation at the transmitter and receiver by using robust iterative DFE. In reference [7], the Zero Forcing (ZF) equalizer investigates the sparseness of the multiple input multiple output channel matrix to minimize the complexity calculations. In reference [8], the banded approximation operation was used to implement a joint equalization and CFO compensation. The issue of CFOs compensation for single carrier systems has been comprehensively explored in several papers. The method proposed in this paper outperforms the conventional methods reported so far.

The principal operation of the proposed equalization is based on the modified Volterra series in which the decision feedback information acquired from the output is included in the equalization operation [9]. As a consequence of the matrix inversion operation, the CFO is removed, and the BER performance is enhanced. The banded matrix operation is used for a reduction of the inter symbol interference (ISI), inter antenna interference (IAI), and noise [10]. The modified Volterra series is capable of explaining a high set of nonlinear system with memory. The traditional Volterra approach for removing ISI uses predistortion at the transmitter and a nonlinear equalization at the receiver. To recover the damaged signal, additional circuitry with a nonlinear signal processing technique and a nonlinear equalizer are used in tandem [11].

Contributions of this paper can be summarized as follows: (i) Deriving an approximate modified Volterra series for ISI noise cancellation, (ii) reducing the BER for uplink LFDM systems with Quadrature Amplitude Modulation (QAM) for AWGN and frequency-selective fading channels (FSFC) using the modified Volterra equalizer, (iii) estimating the reduced complexity required in using the modified Volterra series equations based on the ISI cancellation, (iv) suggesting a reduced complexity CFO compensation technique.

In this paper, a modified Volterra equalization scheme with a banded matrix approximation technique is applied in the LFDMA system for ISI cancellation and computational complexity reduction. The remainder of this paper is organized as follows: Sect. 2 depicts an overview of LFDMA system model. Section 3 outlines the modified Volterra equalization and ISI cancellation scheme in the LFDMA scheme. In Sect. 4 describes the proposed method results by simulation and Sect. 5 provides the paper conclusions.

2   LFDMA System

At the transmitter for the qth user with $q = 1, 2, ..., Q$, the input binary data is passed through a QAM modulation [12]. The modulated output signal is then converted into an N-point Fast Fourier Transform (FFT) symbol mapping, which is followed by LFDMA mapping process. Subcarrier mapping determines the transmission spectrum part, and the mapped signals are again converted into the time domain by using the N-point inverse FFT (IFFT) and it is presumed that each user uses the same bandwidth. The subcarrier mapping of every user can be defined as,

$$X^{(q)} = X_0^{(q)}, ...X_{N-1}^{(q)}\} \tag{1}$$

where $(.)^{(q)}$ represents user 'q' assignment.

$$X_i^{(q)} = \begin{cases} A_i^{(q)} \ for \ 0 \leq i \leq N-1 \\ 0 \qquad otherwise \end{cases} \qquad (2)$$

where, $A_i^{(q)}$ is the symbol transmitted by user 'q' at the carrier 'i'. The output signals are locally mapped on M subcarriers where M > N. By applying IFFT to $X_i^{(q)}$, the time domain signal can be represented as,

$$x^{(q)}(m) = \frac{1}{M} \sum_{l=0}^{L} X_i^{(q)} e^{\frac{j2\pi im}{M}} \qquad (3)$$

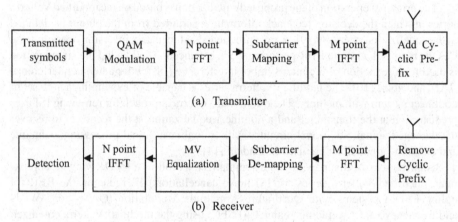

(a) Transmitter

(b) Receiver

Fig. 1. Block representation of LFDMA system model.

After that, the Cyclic Prefix (CP) is inserted at the end of each block to cancel out ISI. The received signal after CP removal is the superposition of every user and it can be represented as,

$$r(m) = \sum_{q=1}^{Q} r^{(q)}(m) + w(m) \qquad (4)$$

where, w(m) is the AWGN channel output vector.

$$r^q(m) = \frac{e^{j2\pi \psi^{(q)}(m)/M}}{M} \sum_{i=P_q} X_i^{(q)} H_i^{(q)} e^{j2\pi im/M} \qquad (5)$$

where $H_i^{(q)}$ is the channel frequency response between base station and user q. The CFO normalized is denoted by $\psi^{(q)} = \Delta g^{(q)}/\Delta G$ where, $\Delta g^{(q)}$ is the Carrier Frequency Offset between base station and user q, ΔG is the intercarrier spacing. Finally, the output of the FFT signal after demodulation is as illustrated in Fig. 1, and it can be expressed as

$$Y_i = R_i + W_i \qquad (6)$$

where W_i is the noise associated with each subcarrier and R_i is given as follows.

$$R_i = \sum_{i' \in P^{(q)}} \sum_{q=1}^{Q} \frac{X_i^{(q)} H_i^{(q)}}{N} \left(\sum_{n=0}^{N-1} e^{j2\pi \frac{(i'-i+\psi^{(q)})n}{N}} \right) \tag{7}$$

3 Modified Volterra Equalizer

For an uplink data transmission, consider the general Volterra equalizer with a decision-feedback equalization (DFE) structure [13]. The equalizer, as illustrated in Fig. 2, creates a nonlinear combination of the Volterra equalizer demodulated complex signal samples and a nonlinear combination of the DFE detected data symbols. Then the two sums are combined before creating the threshold detection. Accordingly, the modified equalizer output is of the form

$$m(i) = \sum_{c=1}^{l} \sum_{c_1=0}^{l_1} \cdots \sum_{c_l=c_{l-1}}^{l_j} a(c_1 \ldots, c_l) \times s(i-c_1) \ldots .s(i-c_l)$$
$$+ \sum_{n=1}^{t} b(n)\omega(i-n) + v(n) \tag{8}$$

where $a(c_1 \ldots, c_l)$ denotes the taps of pth order Volterra kernel, l is the memory length, $v(n)$ is the channel output noise vector, $s(i)$ is the input signal and $m(i)$ is the output signal, decision feedback taps is represented as $b(n)$ and $\omega(i)$ denotes the output of decision block $m(i)$.

3.1 Reduced Complexity of Modified Volterra Equalizer

Consider the 2-kernel modified Volterra approximation of the kth sample result for a modified Volterra equalizer with real valued input signal s, denoted by,

$$m(k) = \sum_{n_1'=0}^{V_1-1} a_1(n_1')s(k-n_1') + \sum_{n_1'=0}^{V_2-1} \sum_{n_2'=0}^{n_1'} a_2(n_1', n_2')s(k-n_1')s(k-n_2)$$
$$+ \sum_{n=1}^{t} b(n)\omega(i-n) + v(n) \tag{9}$$

Here $\sum_{n_1'=0}^{V_1-1} a_1(n_1')s(k-n_1')$ is the linear equalizer with V_1 taps and a_1 weights. $\sum_{n_1'=0}^{V_2-1} \sum_{n_2'=0}^{n_1'} a_2(n_1', n_2')s(k-n_1')s(k-n_2')$ is the nonlinear equalizer with V_2 memory length and a_2 weights [14]. Hence, taps and multiplications required for the 2-kernel proposed equalizer can be calculated as follows.

$$\text{Total number of taps} = V_1 + \frac{V_2(V_2+1)}{2} + T_1 \tag{10}$$

$$\text{Total multiplications} = V_1 + V_2(V_2+1) + T_2 \tag{11}$$

where T_1 is the number of taps of DFE and T_2 is the multiplications required for DFE. The computational complexity of this technique is more by reason of the number of cross-element product necessary for the nonlinear equalizer operation [15]. It is important

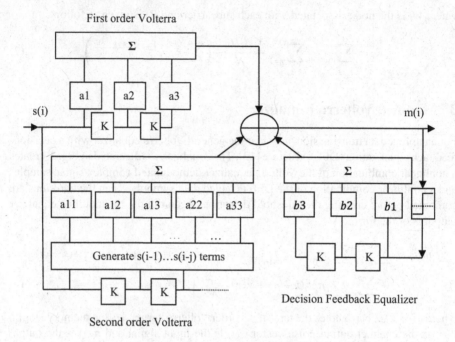

Fig. 2. Block schematic of the Modified Volterra Equalizer.

to devise an effective method for reducing the number of terms while retaining the performance of the recommended equalization scheme. Generally, the diagonal ($n_2' = n_1'$) products are important, as they are related to the impairments that occur from the square-law identification. Hence, a reduced-complexity model of the modified Volterra nonlinear equalizer can be expressed as

$$m(k) = \sum_{n_1'=0}^{V_1-1} a_1(n_1')s(k - n_1') + \sum_{n_2'=0}^{V_2-1} a_2(n_2')s^2(k - n_2')$$
$$+ \sum_{n=1}^{t} b(n)\omega(i - n) + v(n) \tag{12}$$

which is similar to the proposed modified Volterra nonlinear equalizer. The modified equalizer given above requires only $V_1 + V_2 + T_1$ taps and $V_1 + 2V_2 + T_2$ products in total for both linear and nonlinear processes and can be easily modified by a least mean square (LMS) algorithm, which is represented as

$$a_1(k + 1) = a_1(k) + \lambda_1 \psi(k)s_1(k) \tag{13}$$

$$a_2(k + 1) = a_2(k) + \lambda_2 \psi(k)s_2(k) \tag{14}$$

where $\psi(k) = x(k) - m(k)$; a_i, i = [1, 2], represents the coefficients of tap weights, $s_1(k) = [s(k), s(k-1), \ldots s(k-V_1)]$ and $s_2(k) = [s^2(k), s^2(k-1), \ldots s^2(k-V_1)]$ is the vector coefficient of linear and nonlinear equalizer, λ_i is the convergence factor, $\psi(k)$ is the error signal and $s(k)$ is the training sample [16]. The approach proposed for LFDMA uplink transmission is not confined to the $n_2' = n_1'$ situation, since extra multiplication terms such as $n_2' = (n_1' - 1, n_1' - 2...)$ can be widely introduced depending on the system performance or computational complexity demands of the link.

3.2 CFO Compensation

CFO occurs in uplink LFDMA systems as a result of frequency vibrations and mis-alignment in the transmitter or receiver, and it produces interference from nearby sub-carriers [17]. The proposed ISI cancellation technique for nonlinear channels combines the Volterra equalizer and the decision-feedback equalizer to estimate and eliminate ISI from the past and the future data symbols. The cancellation of ISI using the final receiver decisions consists of two parts [18]. The Volterra structure is used initially to subtract from the delayed version of the demodulated signal. The next component is the decision-feedback equalizer, which synthesizes the ISI using the final decisions and subtracts it from the signal at the threshold detector input.

$$r^{(q)} = [r^{(q)}(0), r^{(q)}(1), \ldots r(N-1)]^T \tag{15}$$

Let us consider a diagonal matrix of $N \times N$ of single LFDMA user,

$$D^{(q)} = \text{diagonal}\left\{ 1, \frac{e^{j2\pi \psi^{(q)}}}{N}, \ldots \frac{e^{j2\pi \psi^{(q)}(N-1)}}{N} \right\} \tag{16}$$

$$S^{(q)} = \left[X^{(q)} N_0^{(q)}, X^{(q)} N_1^{(q)}, \ldots, X^{(q)} N_{N-1}^{(q)} \right] \tag{17}$$

G is the $M \times N$ FFT matrix, with elements is represented as,

$$[G]_{u,v} = \frac{1}{\sqrt{N}} e^{-j2\pi (u-1)(v-1)/N} \tag{18}$$

where N number of the signals are used for data transmissionfor $1 \le u \le M$ and $1 \le v \le N$. (4) is written in matrix form as,

$$R = \sum_{q=1}^{Q} R^{(q)} + W \tag{19}$$

where $R^{(q)} = D^{(q)}.G.S^{(q)}$

The ideal signal part of the received signal in frequency domain without CFO is

$$S = [S_{N_{UC}}, \ldots, S_{N-N_{UC}-1}]^T \tag{20}$$

where N_{UC} is the number of unmapped subcarriers of the LFDMA signal and $S_i = \sum_{q=1}^{Q} X_i^{(q)} H_i^{(q)}$ for $N < i < N - N_{UC} - 1$. Let us consider $S^{(q)}$ as the LFDMA uplink signal for every user, which can be written as,

$$S^{(q)} = \delta^{(q)} S \tag{21}$$

where $\delta^{(q)} = diagonal\{\delta_0{}^{(q)}, \ldots \delta_{M-1}{}^{(q)}\}$

$$\delta_i{}^{(q)} = \begin{array}{l} 1 \; \; if \; i \in P^{(q)} \\ 0 \; \; otherwise \end{array} \tag{22}$$

After demodulation, the LFDMA signal can be written as,

$$y = \alpha + z, \tag{23}$$

where $\alpha = \sum_{q=1}^{Q} GD^{(q)}G^H s^{(q)}$ and z is the noise associated. Denoting $\varphi^{(q)} = GD^{(q)}G^H$ and substituting in (9), the actual receive signal α can be written as,

$$\alpha = \sum_{q=1}^{Q} \varphi^{(q)}s^{(q)} = \varphi s \tag{24}$$

where $\varphi = \sum_{q=1}^{Q} \varphi^{(q)}\delta^{(q)}$. The term φ refers to an interference matrix associated with the original received LFDMA signal with CFO. The ISI for each user is described by the matrix form as [19],

$$[\varphi^q]_{u,v} = \frac{1}{N} \frac{1 - e^{j2\pi(u-v+\psi^{(q)})}}{1 - e^{j2\pi(u-v+\psi^{(q)})/N}} \tag{25}$$

for $1 \leq u, v \leq M$, where M is the carrier for data transmission and $\psi^{(q)}$ is the normalized CFO $\psi^{(q)} = \Delta o^{(q)}/\Delta d$, where $\Delta o^{(q)}$ is the CFO between user q and base station and Δd is the intercarrier spacing. The matrix with banded structure can be represented as

$$[\varphi_\gamma]_{u,v} = \begin{cases} [\varphi]_{u,v} \; \; if \; |u-v| \leq \gamma \\ 0 \; \; \; \; \; if \; |u-v| > \gamma \end{cases} \tag{26}$$

where γ denotes the matrix bandwidth. To eliminate the elements with large interference signals, the periodic structure is $[\varphi]$, $\gamma \leq 2M$, where M is the number of subcarriers. Banded matrix inverse requires very low computation compared with a complete matrix inversion. Therefore, this approximation allows a tradeoff between the low computational complexity and the interference cancellation. To compensate the CFO effect, the proposed estimation technique is utilized to find the estimate of s represented as s'. The minimum mean squared error (MMSE) estimation can be written as,

$$s' = \varphi_\gamma{}^H (\varphi_\gamma{}^H \varphi_\gamma + Q^2 I)y \tag{27}$$

where $Q^2 = \frac{\sigma_z^2}{\sigma_s^2}$ indicates average power level. The Eq. (27) cancells out the interferences caused by the effect of CFO.

4 Simulation Results and Discussion

MATLAB simulation is carried out to evaluate the proposed modified Volterra equalizer technique. The simulation settings and parameters for the LFDMA uplink transmission are shown in Table 1.

CFO's BER performance in multipath impaired LFDMA is compared with that of unimpaired LFDMA in Fig. 3. Volterra equalization and modified Volterra equalization techniques are used at the LFDMA receiver to eliminate the channel effects. Unimpaired LFDMA requires an SNR of 30 dB to achieve BER of 10^{-5}. Furthermore, in this figure, the performance of LFDMA with modified Volterra is shown to be superior to conventional approaches such as circular convolution, single user detection, and Iterative MMSE. Inversion of the Banded Matrix decreases ISI authority and frames the LFDMA system less susceptible to CFO errors. Moreover, the enhanced Volterra equalizer estimates and compensates for the receiver noise, improving BER performance. The graph clearly illustrates that the proposed LFDMA requires less SNR to attain the same BER performance compared to the existing multipath impaired LFDMA approaches.

Table 1. Simulation parameters

Parameters	Description
FFT block size	128
Channel type	AWGN, Rayleigh
IFFT size	256
Cyclic prefix rate	1/16
Modulation	QAM (16 and 64)
Subcarrier mapping	LFDMA
System bandwidth	5 MHz
Equalizer type	MV

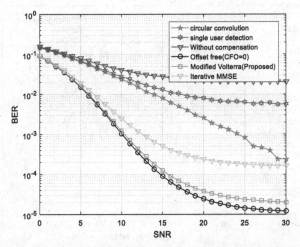

Fig. 3. BER performance of an LFDMA system with and without multipath impairments is compared using the conventional technique and the proposed modified Volterra equalisation.

Figure 4 states that under normalised CFO values, the proposed method ISI similarity of LFDMA with multicarrier OFDM system and existing LFDMA ranges from 0 to 0.5.

The graph clearly illustrates that the proposed system outperforms than the other two in terms of ISI reduction. The ISI obtained from the proposed LFDMA, existing LFDMA, and OFDM at a normalized CFO of 0.25 obtained are −25 dB, −16 dB, and −7 dB. The lower ISI obtained by the modified Volterra technique LFDMA helps to improve the overall system performance effectively. The side lobe levels of the proposed LFDMA, existing LFDMA and OFDM are −48 dB, −40 dBand −32 dB, respectively.

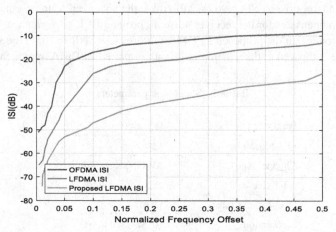

Fig. 4. Proposed LFDMA's ISI performance is compared with that of OFDM and conventional LFDMA.

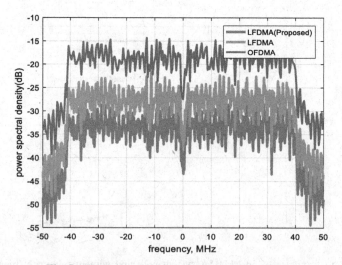

Fig. 5. Comparison of PSD of the proposed LFDMA

The PSD graph reveals that the proposed LFDMA has lower ISI than traditional LFDMA and OFDM due to its reduced side lobes, as shown in Fig. 5. Figure 6 shows the capacity of proposed LFDMA system for AWGN and FSFC under different transmit-receive antenna.

Figure 7 describes the difference of computational complexity for the proposed method with respect to memory length. From the figure, it can be seen that the total number of multiplications to implement the modified Volterra equalizer increases as the memory length increases.

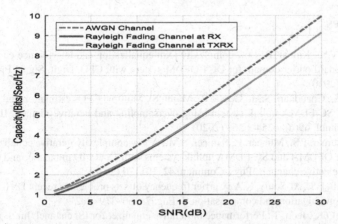

Fig. 6. Proposed LFDMA system capacity for various TX-RX antenna for AWGN and Rayleigh channel

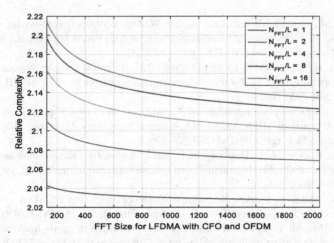

Fig. 7. Computational complexity comparison between the proposed LFDMA and OFDM.

5 Conclusion

The work of multipath disability on the LFDMA system performance is analyzed in this paper. The demand for CFO compensation strategies in the uplink LFDMA transmission system is determined. This paper introduces a low-complexity technique using a novel equalization methodology to minimize CFO with banded matrix approximation. As a result, the overall BER performance of the LFDMA system has improved. The results determined that the proposed multipath impairments adjusted LFDMA system is a viable approach for improving the performance of the uplink transmission system and it is superior to the techniques reported so far.

References

1. Trivedi, V.K., Kumar, P.: Low complexity joint equalization and interference compensation in fractional Fourier domain for DCT-OFDM system with CFO. Digit. Signal Process. **107**, 102863 (2020)
2. Kumar, S., Chaudhari, S.M., Gupta, R., Majhi, S.: Multiple CFOs estimation and implementation of SC-FDMA uplink system using oversampling and iterative method. IEEE Trans. Veh. Technol. **69**(6), 6254–6263 (2020)
3. Sanoopkumar, P.S., Muneer, P., Sameer, S.M.: A low complexity iterative equalization technique for OFDMA and SC-FDMA uplink systems with Tx-Rx IQ imbalance and CFO under doubly selective channels. Phys. Commun. **42**, 101170 (2020)
4. Al-kamali, F.S., Al-Soufy, K.A.: Carrier frequency offsets problem in recent DST-SC-FDMA system: investigation and compensation. J. Eng. **7**, 366–379 (2021)
5. Nguyen, Q.K., Jeon, T.: Performance of iterative equalizer for ISI channel. Int. J. Adv. Smart Converg. **9**(3), 141–144 (2020)
6. Iqbal, N., Zerguine, A., Alouini, M.S.: A robust frequency domain decision feedback equalization system for uplink SC-FDMA systems. IEEE Trans. Wirel. Commun. **20**, 8110–8118 (2021)
7. Shehata, M., Wang, K., Withayachumnankul, W.: Low-complexity zero-forcing equalization for MIMO SC-FDMA terahertz communications. In: 2021 Fourth International Workshop on Mobile Terahertz Systems (IWMTS), pp. 1–5 (2021)
8. Ramadan, K., Dessouky, M.I., Abd El-Samie, F.E.: Joint low-complexity equalisation and CFO compensation for DCT–OFDM communication systems based on SIC. IET Commun. **14**(20), 3549–3559 (2020)
9. Selvaraj, K., Judson, D., Ganeshkumar, P., Anandaraj, M.: Low complexity linear detection for uplink multiuser MIMO SC-FDMA systems. Wirel. Pers. Commun. **112**(1), 631–649 (2020). https://doi.org/10.1007/s11277-020-07065-z
10. Ramadan, K., Alturki, A., Dessouky, M.I., Abd El-Samie, F.E.: Equalization and CFO compensation for SISO-OFDM communication systems with chaotic interleaving. Int. J. Electron. **108**, 1590–1609 (2021)
11. Soufy, A., Abdullah, K.: An efficient transmission of image over SC-FDMA system in the presence of CFO. J. Commun. Technol. Electron. Comput. Sci. **18**, 8–18 (2018)
12. Deepak, P.M., Ali, C.K.: Sensitivity of filter bank SCFDMA to carrier frequency offset and its compensation using firefly algorithm. Int. J. Commun Syst **31**(14), e3743 (2018)
13. Liu, N., Cheng, J.: Blind I/Q imbalance and nonlinear ISI mitigation in Nyquist-SCM direct detection system with cascaded widely linear and Volterra equalizer. Opt. Commun. **409**, 94–98 (2018)
14. Diamantopoulos, N.P., Kobayashi, W., Nishi, H., Takeda, K., Kakitsuka, T., Matsuo, S.: 56-Gb/s VSB-PAM-4 over 80-km using 1550-nm EA-DFB laser and reduced-complexity nonlinear equalization. In: 2017 European Conference on Optical Communication (ECOC), pp. 1–3. IEEE (2017)

15. Mrabet, H., Mhatli, S.: A reduced complexity Volterra-based nonlinear equalizer for up to 100 Gb/s coherent optical communications. Optoelectron. Adv. Mater. Rapid Commun. **12**(3–4), 186–192 (2018)
16. Angelotti, A.M., Gibiino, G.P., Santarelli, A.: Efficient implementation of a modified-Volterra radio-frequency power amplifier nonlinear dynamic model by global rational functions approximation. Int. J. RF Microw. Comput. Aided Eng. **30**(11), e22392 (2020)
17. Liu, N., Cheng, J., Li, C.: Nonlinear ISI cancellation in Nyquist-SCM direct detection PON downstream scheme with Volterra pre-equalizer. Opt. Fiber Technol. **45**, 14–18 (2018)
18. Li, D., et al.: Amplifier-free 4×96 Gb/s PAM8 transmission enabled by modified Volterra equalizer for short-reach applications using directly modulated lasers. Opt. Express **27**(13), 17927–17939 (2019)
19. González, G.J., Gregorio, F.H., Cousseau, J.E.: Carrier frequency offset compensation for OFDMA systems using circular banded matrices. Lat. Am. Appl. Res. **43**, 255–260 (2013)

DICCh-D: Detecting IPv6-Based Covert Channels Using DNN

Arti Dua[1]([⊠]) [iD], Vinita Jindal[2] [iD], and Punam Bedi[3] [iD]

[1] Bhaskaracharya College of Applied Sciences, University of Delhi, Delhi, India
arti.batra@bcas.du.ac.in
[2] Keshav Mahavidyalaya, University of Delhi, Delhi, India
vjindal@keshav.du.ac.in
[3] Department of Computer Science, University of Delhi, Delhi, India
pbedi@cs.du.ac.in

Abstract. Stegomalware uses Information hiding techniques within Network protocols to leak out sensitive data and/or to exchange hidden commands between secretly communicating parties. Internet Protocol version 6 (IPv6) is a network layer protocol that is rapidly replacing Internet Protocol version 4 (IPv4). This has resulted in an increase in the availability of IPv6 packets over the internet, thereby making IPv6 a good candidate for the establishment of Network covert channels (NCCs). NCCs use either network flows or network packets to communicate in a hidden way such that no one notices the presence of secret information inside them. This secret information can be injected into network flows or network packets in the inter-packet delays and/or in any of the redundant, unused, reserved storage areas of the packets. Substantial research work has already been done in the area of covert channel detection in IPv4. Now, with IPv6 taking over the internet, the focus has shifted towards the detection of possible covert channels in IPv6. Thus this paper proposes DICCh-D, a model for the Detection of IPv6-based Covert Channels using DNN. For experimentation, the dataset was constructed using normal IPv6 packets obtained from CAIDA's dataset and covert IPv6 packets created by running an IPv6-based covert packets generation tool. The proposed method outperforms CNN, LSTM and SVM in terms of accuracy with acceptable training and testing time. DICCh-D attained an accuracy of 99.59% and a recall value of 0.99, which is better than the existing technique used in literature.

Keywords: Network covert channel detection · Stegomalware · IPv6 · CAIDA dataset · Deep neural network

1 Introduction

With the growth of technology, the attackers have started using sophisticated and new techniques to perform various attacks like crypto lockers, advanced persistent threats (APT), etc. Stegomalware concerns the transfer of malware through some form of Information hiding and is being used by attackers extensively [1]. Stegomalware offers hidden

C. Badica et al. (Eds.): ICICCT 2022, CCIS 1670, pp. 42–53, 2022.
https://doi.org/10.1007/978-3-031-20977-2_4

transfer of malware in legitimate Internet traffic flows offering reasonable undetectability. Network covert channels (NCCs) utilize network protocols for Information Hiding that can further be used as a medium for performing above mentioned attacks. NCCs can be categorized into three types:

1. Storage-Based Network Covert Channels: These NCCs utilize the storage area of the header or payload part of a protocol to hide secret information.
2. Timing-Based Network Covert Channels: These types of NCCs utilize the inter-packet delays between consecutive packets to hide secret information.
3. Hybrid Network Covert Channels: These types of NCCs utilize both storage and timing-based Network covert channels simultaneously.

The efficiency of any NCC depends upon three characteristics:

1. Information hiding capacity of the covert channel
2. The undetectability of the hidden information
3. The robustness of the hiding algorithm used to develop NCC.

The usability of the Network protocol used in the NCC also affects the Information hiding capacity of the NCC. The Network protocols that have higher usability over the networks offer higher covert capacity. With IPv6 rapidly replacing IPv4 over the Internet, the usability of IPv6 packets over the internet is also increasing day by day. This makes IPv6 a good target for hidden communication. Some of the possible storage-based network covert channels that may be developed using the IPv6 protocol have been proposed by researchers in [2, 3]. A lot of work has already been done on the detection of IPv4-based covert channels. To the best of our knowledge, the area of IPv6-based covert channel detection is comparatively less explored. Thus this paper proposes DICCh-D, a model to detect IPv6-based covert channels using Deep Neural Network. For experimentation, the dataset was created using normal IPv6 packets obtained from CAIDA's dataset of Anonymized Internet Traces 2019 [4] and covert IPv6 packets generated by running the pcapStego tool [5].

The further organization of this paper is as follows. Section 2 briefly discusses the IPv6 Protocol and the Deep Neural Network. In Sect. 3, the related research work done in the area of detection of IPv6-based NCCs is discussed. Section 4 elaborates on the details and working of the proposed DICCh-D. Section 5 discusses the construction of the dataset, experiments, and results followed by Sect. 6 which concludes this paper.

2 Background Information

This section gives a brief description of IPv6 Protocol and the Deep Neural Network algorithm which are used in this paper.

2.1 Internet Protocol Version 6

The Internet Engineering Task Force (IETF) developed version 6 of the Internet Protocol in the year 1998 to overcome the problem of exhausting 32 bits long IPv4 addresses.

RFC 8200 [6] provides a detailed description of the IPv6 protocol. It is soon expected to take over its prevalent predecessor IPv4 and is termed the next-generation protocol. According to Google statistics, the adoption rate for IPv6 reached a value of 37.25% on January 15, 2022, which is continuously increasing [7]. The header structure of this protocol is depicted in Fig. 1 below.

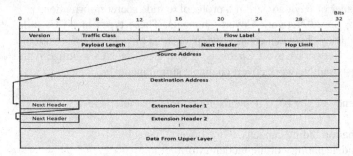

Fig. 1. Header structure of IPv6 protocol

The first field in the header is the Version field. It is 4 bits long and contains the version number of the Internet Protocol being used. For IPv6 packets, the value of this field is fixed to 6. The second field in the IPv6 header is the Traffic Class (TC) field. This field is 1 byte long and is used for Network Traffic Management. The subsequent field in the IPv6 header is the Flow Label (FL) field whose size is 20 bits long and is used to identify the packets belonging to a single flow. The fourth field in the sequence is the Payload Length (PL) field which is 2 bytes long in size and stores the length of both the extension headers (if any) and the data from the upper layer protocols. Next comes, a 1-byte long Next Header (NH) field that stores the protocol number of the extension header attached next to the fixed IPv6 header. Extension headers (EH) like Hop by Hop EH, Destination EH, Routing EH, Fragmentation EH, Authentication EH, and Encrypted Payload Security EH are some extension headers specified in RFC 8200 [6]. The common upper layer extension headers are the Transmission Control Protocol header and User Datagram Protocol header. The next field in the IPv6 header is a 1 byte long Hop Limit (HL) field that defines the number of nodes that an IPv6 packet can traverse without getting discarded over the Internet. Next to it are Source and Destination Address Field. Both of these fields are 128 bits long and hold the logical source and destination address of an IPv6 packet. Amongst all the header fields of IPv6, the highest storage-based covert capacity is offered by the Flow Label field which is 20 bits. Further, the Traffic class field also offers a good hiding capacity of 8 bits per IPv6 packet. The randomness in the legitimate values of these two fields makes them suitable candidates for covert channel creation.

2.2 DNN Model

A DNN is a machine learning algorithm. It is a special type of neural network with three types of layers: Input Layer L_i (One in number), Hidden Layers L_{H1}, L_{H2}, ... L_{HN}

(two or more in number), and Output Layer L_o (One in number). Every layer contains a certain number of neurons. Further, a neuron at one layer is connected to every other neuron at the next layer in the forward direction making it a feed-forward network and each of these connections is assigned some weight W_{xy}. There is no connection between neurons at the same layer. During the training phase of a model, the algorithm tries to find the best weight for each connection through back-propagation. The training of a DNN starts with the input layer. Each neuron at this layer receives input and multiplies this received value with the initial weights assigned to its connection with neurons at the next layer. Further, these product values are forwarded to the hidden layer, L_{H1} where a non-linear activation function is applied to the weighted input value received at each neuron, from the previous layer. In this way, each subsequent hidden layer extracts more significant information. The hidden layer L_{HN} processes the information and forwards it finally to the output layer L_o which gives a probability of the current input belonging to the available classes/labels. If the class with the highest probability value for this input does not match the corresponding actual class, the output value is sent back to the initial layers to adjust the errors and update the weights again.

After the completion of the training phase, the final weights of the DNN are used to make predictions on the testing data to test the generalization capability of the trained model.

3 Related Work

The idea of the development of covert channels over Network communication protocol was first given by Handel and Sandford in the year 1996 [8]. In this work, the authors discussed how various network protocols operating at various layers of the OSI model can be exploited for developing covert channels for secret and hidden communications. Over the years, various researchers also proposed several techniques for the development of covert channels over different network protocols used over the LANs (Local Area Network) and the Internet including IPv4, TCP, UDP, ARP, ICMP [9–14]. Comparatively, IPv6 being a younger protocol was explored by Lucena et al. [2] in the year 2005 for the possibility of the development of covert channels. The authors suggested the possibility of 22 different storage-based covert channels using different parts of the IPv6 header. In 2019, Mazurczyk et al. practically experimented with the possibility and actual bandwidth of covert channels proposed by Lucena et al. over the internet [3]. The authors used the following six IPv6 header fields individually to develop covert channels namely Traffic Class, Flow Label, Payload Length, Next Header, Hop Limit, and Source Address field. Bedi et al. proposed an IPv6-based covert channel that utilized the presence/absence of an extension header in a fixed predefined order to covertly convey a 0/1 bit at respective positions [15].

Further, this paper discusses the work done in the detection of IPv6-based Network covert channels. In 2006, Lewandowski et al. suggested the elimination of covert channels based on Routing extension headers and Hop Limit using Traffic normalization with the help of active wardens in IPv6 networks [16]. In [17], Luca et al. suggested the use of code augmentation in extended Berkeley Packet Filter (eBPF) within Linux kernel to collect the statistics of IPv6 header fields. Repetto et al. suggested the use of the BCC tool for running eBPF programs to obtain statistics about three specific header fields in IPv6 viz. Flow Label, Traffic Class, and Hop Limit [18]. The authors inferred that abnormal changes in the statistical values of these header fields can raise an alarm about the presence of a covert channel. But this eBPF-based covert channel detection mechanism gives good accuracy with more granular values of the number of bins which consumes a large amount of resources. Also, short covert communications cannot be detected using the same mechanism. Salih et al. used a Naive Bayes classifier which is a Machine Learning technique to detect IPv6-based covert channels with an accuracy of 94.47% [19]. They proposed a framework that uses a hybrid method for feature selection that uses Intelligent Heuristic Algorithm (IHA) in addition to a modified Decision Tree C4.5 to create primary training data to detect hidden channels in the IPv6 network. AI Senaid in his work [20] applied a CNN-based approach to identify covert channel created in the code field of ICMPv6 protocol. To the best of our knowledge, there is a scope for improvement in prediction accuracy or resource consumption for the detection of IPv6-based covert channels. Thus, in this paper, DICCh-D, a model to detect IPv6-based covert channels using DNN is proposed. The next section describes the proposed detection model.

4   The Proposed DICCh-D

This paper proposes DICCh-D, a model that detects IPv6-based covert channels using DNN. The development of DICCh-D is divided into three phases as shown in Fig. 2. The first phase creates the IPv6 packets dataset containing both covert and normal IPv6 packets. The second phase extracts the header fields of these IPv6 packets to create a new dataset of header fields of covert and normal IPv6 packets. In the third phase, the training and validation datasets are used to train and validate the DNN whereas the testing dataset is used to test the generalization capability of the trained model. Each of the phases is explained further in the sub-sections.

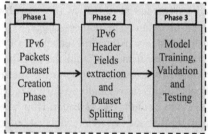

Fig. 2. Development framework of proposed DICCh-D

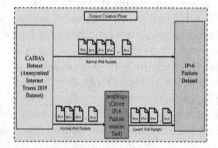

Fig. 3. IPv6 packets dataset creation phase

4.1   Phase 1: IPv6 Packets Dataset Creation

The IPv6 packet dataset consisted of normal IPv6 packets and covert IPv6 packets. The process of dataset creation is shown in Fig. 3. The normal IPv6 packets were obtained randomly from CAIDA's Anonymized Internet Traces 2019 [4].

The covert IPv6 packets were created with the help of a tool called pcapStego [5]. This tool offers the creation of storage-based covert packets in IPv6 header fields. After the creation of the IPv6 packets dataset containing normal IPv6 packets and covert IPv6 packets, the next step was the extraction of IPv6 header fields to create a new dataset.

4.2 Phase 2: Extraction of IPv6 Header Fields from IPv6 Packets Dataset

A Network protocol packet consists of two vital components, a packet header, and a payload. A packet header contains the metadata about the current packet and the payload part contains the actual information carried by the packet over a network. In this paper, only the detection of storage-based network covert channels over IPv6 is considered. Normal IPv6 packets were obtained from Anonymized Internet Traces 2019 obtained from CAIDA [4]. The covert IPv6 packets were created with the help of a tool named pcapStego [5]. The .pcap files for both normal and covert data packets were obtained and the following header fields were fetched from these packets: Flow Label, Traffic Class, Payload Length, Hop Limit, Next Header, Source IPv6 address, Destination IPv6 Address, Source Port, Destination Port, Transport Layer Protocol. The task of extraction of IPv6 header fields was done with the help of the Wireshark tool [21]. After this, the headers of normal IPv6 packets and headers of covert IPv6 were combined together to form a complete dataset with labels. Subsequently, the complete dataset was divided into the training_and_validate dataset (80% of the complete dataset) and the testing dataset (20% of the complete dataset).

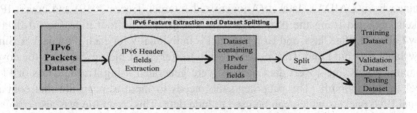

Fig. 4. IPv6 header fields extraction

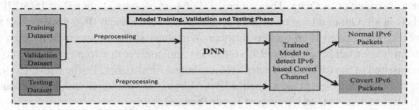

Fig. 5. Model training, validation and testing phase

The training_and_validate dataset was further split into the training dataset (90% of the training_and_validate dataset) and validation dataset (10% of the training_and_validate dataset) to check the performance of the DNN after each epoch on the validation dataset while training the DNN. The complete working of this phase is shown in Fig. 4.

4.3 Phase 3: Dataset Preprocessing, Training and Testing of the DNN

In this phase, three subtasks of dataset preprocessing, training, and testing the DNN are performed as shown in Fig. 5. Before the training phase, the training dataset and the validation dataset are preprocessed to quantize and standardize the data. This preprocessed training dataset is used to train the DNN. The structure of the DNN consisted of one input layer, three hidden layers (with 24, 12, and 6 neurons), and one output layer. The activation function used at the hidden layers was Rectified Linear Unit (ReLU). The activation function used at the output layer was sigmoid. The values fed to the output layer of the DNN are converted to respective values between 0 and 1 with the help of the sigmoid activation function to make the predictions.

5 Experimental Study

The proposed DICCh-D was developed using a 1.8 GHz Dual-Core Intel Core i5 processor on macOS Catalina. Python version 3.6.8 was used for the development of the proposed DICCh-D. The development of DICCh-D consisted of the creation of a dataset, preprocessing of the dataset, training of the DNN, and testing of the DNN.

5.1 Dataset

The dataset for training and testing of the DICCh-D consisted of normal IPv6 packets obtained from CAIDA's dataset (Anonymized Internet Traces 2019) and covert IPv6 packets obtained using the pcapStego tool. The pcapStego tool hides covert data in Flow Label, Traffic Class, and Hop limit fields individually for each IPv6 packet. Since Flow label (20 bits) and Traffic class (8 bits) offer good hiding capacity for covert communications, the covert data packets were generated using Traffic Class or Flow Label fields randomly. The pcapStego tool needs to input a .pcap file that contains normal IPv6 packets which can be used to hide data. This .pcap file was also obtained from CAIDA's Anonymized Internet Traces IPv6 2019 dataset. The final combined IPv6 packets dataset was then created by combining the normal IPv6 packets and IPv6 packets carrying covert data. The combined IPv6 packets dataset contained 16091 IPv6 packets in all. Out of a total of 16091 packets, 9460 were normal IPv6 packets, and the rest 6631 were covert IPv6 packets. Further, Wireshark software was used to fetch the relevant header fields of captured IPv6 packets and convert that to a.csv file. This.csv file consisted of the following header field attributes: Flow Label, Traffic Class, Payload Length, Hop Limit, Next Header, Source IPv6 address, Destination IPv6 Address, Source Port, Destination Port, and Transport Layer Protocol.

Testing the generalizability of a trained model is an important aspect in assuring how a model will perform on the data it has never seen earlier. For this, the complete dataset of 16091 packets was divided into two parts, the training_and_validation dataset, and the testing dataset. The training_and_validation dataset consisted of 12872 packets and the testing dataset consisted of 3219 packets. The training_and_validation dataset contained 7584 normal IPv6 packets and 5288 covert IPv6 packets. The testing dataset contained 1876 normal packets and 1343 covert IPv6 packets. The first dataset was used to train and validate the model. The second dataset was used to test the generalization ability of the model trained with the first dataset. The preprocessing of both of these datasets was done independently using the same python program to quantize and standardize the values. Section 5.2 describes the preprocessing applied to both datasets separately.

5.2 Preprocessing

In this work, the following steps were done using a python program to preprocess the datasets containing normal and covert IPv6 packets. Firstly, a single attribute corresponding to the Source IPv6 Address field having colon-separated 8 octets was broken into 8 different attributes. Similarly, the Destination IPv6 address was broken down into 8 different attributes. The dataset contained two categorical attributes: Protocol and Next Header. Quantization was used to convert these categorical values into a unique number corresponding to different values of each attribute. Input attributes have different scales and hence there is a need for scaling or standardization in ML algorithms. In this work, *standardscalar()* of *sklearn* library from python was used to scale all the data. The next sub-section describes the training and testing Phase of the proposed DICCh-D.

5.3 Training and Testing Phase

Before starting with the training phase, the preprocessing of the training_and_validation dataset and the testing dataset was done separately. At the beginning of the training phase, the preprocessed training_and_validation dataset was divided into two parts: the training dataset (used solely for the purpose of training the DNN) and the validation dataset (to check the performance of the model after each epoch during the training phase). During the training phase of any Machine learning/Deep Learning algorithm, certain hyperparameters values need to be set such as the number of layers used for training a model, the number of neurons used in each layer of the model, the batch size, the learning rate, the number of epochs needed for training, the optimizer, and the activation function used at each layer. These hyperparameters have to be chosen carefully as it has a significant effect on the performance of the model. Hence the DNN was trained with different configurations like 2, 3, 4 number of hidden layers, the batch size of 10, 32, and the number of epochs from 30 to 50 with an interval of 10. The most optimal hyper-parameters were then decided as the final configuration as follows: number of hidden layers as 3, number of neurons at three hidden layers as 24, 12, and 6 respectively, and the activation function used at the hidden layers was ReLU. At the output layer, the sigmoid activation function was used. The batch size was fixed at 10 and the number of epochs was fixed at 30. The optimizer used was AdamOptimizer. The evaluation metrics used for the evaluation of the DICCh-D are described in Subsect. 5.4.

5.4 Evaluation Metrics

To measure the effectiveness of the proposed DICCh-D, metrics like accuracy, precision, recall, and F1-score were calculated for the testing dataset that was used to check the generalizability of the proposed model. True Positives (TP) is the number of samples classified correctly by a model. False Positives (FP) depicts the number of samples mistakenly classified as being positive by a model. True Negatives (TN) denotes the number of samples which are correctly classified by a model as being negative. False Negatives (FN) depicts the number of samples which are incorrectly classified as being negative. Accuracy describes the total number of samples which are correctly classified by the model. Precision denotes the number of samples actually belonging to a class out of all the samples that were predicted by a model as belonging to that class. Recall is defined as the number of samples correctly predicted by a model out of all the samples belonging to that class. F1-Score is defined as the harmonic mean of the Recall and Precision value. Equations (1) to (4) are used to calculate the Accuracy, Precision, Recall, and F1-Score of a model.

$$Accuracy = \frac{TP + TN}{TP + FP + TN + FN} \tag{1}$$

$$Precision = \frac{TP}{TP + FP} \tag{2}$$

$$Recall = \frac{TP}{TP + FN} \tag{3}$$

$$F1 - Score = \frac{2 * Precision * Recall}{Precision + Recall} \tag{4}$$

The evaluation results of all experiments done using the above-mentioned metrics for different configurations of models in consideration are discussed in the next sub-section.

5.5   Results

The performance of DICCh-D was compared with state-of-the-art Deep-Learning algorithms (CNN, LSTM) and a Machine Learning algorithm (SVM). The CNN was experimented with three different configurations of 1, 2, and 3 1D-Convolutional layer(s), each with a batch size of 10, adopting AdamOptimizer as the optimizer and iterated over 50 epochs. Next, the LSTM model was iterated over 25 epochs each time for three configurations of 1, 2, and 3 LSTM layer(s). Finally, the SVM model was experimented with four different kernel values viz. Linear, sigmoid, polynomial, and RBF. The proposed DICCh-D was experimented with three different configurations of DNN each having 2, 3, and 4 hidden layers respectively. The results for accuracy for each of the classifiers taking different hyperparameters are shown in Fig. 6.

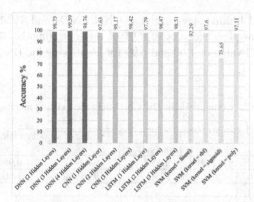

Fig. 6. Performance comparison based on accuracy of DNN, LSTM, CNN and SVM models

Further, the recall, precision, and F1-score values for each of the classifiers taking different hyperparameters each time are shown in Table 1.

Table 1. Performance comparison of DNN, LSTM, CNN and, SVM models with different configurations on the created dataset.

Model	Training Time (s)	Prediction Time(s)	Accuracy %	Precision		Recall		F1-Score	
				Normal	Covert	Normal	Covert	Normal	Covert
DNN (3 Hidden Layers)	54.76	0.30	**99.59**	0.99	1.00	1.00	0.99	1.00	1.00
DNN (2 Hidden Layers)	52.81	0.22	98.75	0.98	1.00	1.00	0.97	0.99	0.98
DNN (4 Hidden Layers)	59.20	0.32	98.76	0.98	1.00	1.00	0.97	0.99	0.98
LSTM (1 Layer)	334	0.93	97.79	0.96	1.00	1.00	0.95	0.98	0.97
LSTM (2 Layers)	634.38	1.69	98.47	0.98	1.00	1.00	0.97	0.99	0.98
LSTM (3 Layers)	955.28	2.76	98.51	0.98	0.99	1.00	0.97	0.99	0.98
CNN (1 Layer)	123.70	0.30	97.63	0.96	1.00	1.00	0.94	0.98	0.97
CNN (2 Layers)	168.69	0.37	98.167	0.97	1.00	1.00	0.96	0.98	0.98
CNN (3 Layers)	312.58	0.48	98.42	0.97	1.00	1.00	0.96	0.99	0.98
SVM (Kernel = linear)	4.34	0.23	92.29	0.89	0.98	0.99	0.84	0.94	0.90
SVM (Kernel = rbf)	**0.617**	0.39	97.6	0.96	1.00	1.00	0.94	0.98	0.97
SVM (Kernel = sigmoid)	3.17	0.55	75.65	0.75	0.76	0.86	0.59	0.80	0.66
SVM (Kernel = poly)	0.94	**0.158**	97.11	0.96	0.99	1.00	0.94	0.98	0.96

The proposed DICCh-D (DNN with 3 hidden layers) took slightly more time than some of its counterparts but in terms of accuracy it clearly outperformed the DNN algorithm with 2 and 4 hidden layers, and all CNN, LSTM and SVM configurations in consideration. It showed an accuracy of 99.59% on the testing dataset, and recorded a precision and a recall value of 1.00 and 0.99 for identifying the IPv6 packets carrying covert data.

Table 2. Comparison of DICCh-D with the existing technique

Model	Training Time (s)	Accuracy(%)	Precision	Recall
Naïve Bayes by Salih et al [19]	**0.15**	94.47%	0.960	0.985
Proposed DICCh-D	52.81	**99.59%**	**1.00**	**0.99**

Salih et al. used a Naive Bayes classifier to detect IPv6-based covert channels with an accuracy of 94.47% [19]. They proposed a framework that uses a hybrid feature selection technique using Intelligent Heuristic Algorithm (IHA) in addition to a modified Decision Tree C4.5 to create primary training data to detect hidden channels in the IPv6 network. A comparison of DICCh-D with the same, in terms of training time, accuracy, precision, and recall is shown in Table 2. Although DICCh-D takes a longer time to train in comparison to the framework proposed by Salih et al., it surely outperforms the same in terms of accuracy, precision, and recall values.

6 Conclusion

In this paper, DICCh-D, a model that detects IPv6-based covert channels using a DNN has been proposed. The dataset needed to train, validate and test DICCh-D was developed using normal IPv6 packets taken from CAIDA's Anonymized Internet Traces 2019 dataset and the covert IPv6 packets. The covert IPv6 packets were generated using the pcapStego tool for hiding data in the Traffic Class and Flow Label fields in the headers of IPv6 packets. Moreover, for testing the generalization ability of the proposed DICCh-D, a testing dataset was kept aside before the model creation and validation phase. The proposed DICCh-D obtained an accuracy of 99.59% and precision and recall rate of 1.00 and 0.99 respectively for identifying IPv6 packets with covert data in the testing dataset. When compared with the state-of-the-art Deep Learning methods like CNN and LSTM, DICCh-D gave better results in terms of time taken for training and testing with comparable accuracy, precision, and recall values. The proposed DICCh-D also outperformed SVM in terms of accuracy.

References

1. Mazurczyk, W., Caviglione, L.: Information hiding as a challenge for malware detection. IEEE Secur. Priv. 2(13), 89–93 (2015)
2. Lucena, N.B., Lewandowski, G., Chapin, S.J.: Covert channels in IPv6. In: Danezis, G., Martin, D. (eds.) PET 2005. LNCS, vol. 3856, pp. 147–166. Springer, Heidelberg (2006). https://doi.org/10.1007/11767831_10

3. Mazurczyk, W., Powojski, K., Caviglione L.: IPv6 covert channels in the wild. In: Proceedings of the Third Central European Cybersecurity Conference, pp. 1–6 (2019)
4. The CAIDA UCSD Anonymized Internet Traces Dataset - [20 Jan 2019, 21 Jan 2019], Center for Applied Internet Data Analysis (2021). https://www.caida.org/data/passive/passive_dataset. Accessed 20 Dec 2021
5. Zuppelli, M., Caviglione, L.: pcapStego - a tool for generating traffic traces for experimenting with network covert channels. In: The 16th International Conference on Availability, Reliability and Security, pp. 1–8 (2021)
6. Deering, S., Hinden, R.: Internet Protocol, Version 6 (Specifications). Internet Engineering Task Force. https://tools.ietf.org/html/rfc8200#section-6. Accessed 10 Dec 2021
7. Google: Google IPv6 (2022). https://www.google.com/intl/en/ipv6/statistics.html#tab=ipv6-adoption. Accessed 15 Jan 2022
8. Handel, T.G., Sandford, M.T.: Hiding data in the OSI network model. In: Anderson, R. (ed.) IH 1996. LNCS, vol. 1174, pp. 23–38. Springer, Heidelberg (1996). https://doi.org/10.1007/3-540-61996-8_29
9. Bedi, P., Dua, A.: Network steganography using the overflow field of timestamp option in an IPv4 packet. Procedia Comput. Sci. **171**, 1810–1818 (2020)
10. Giffin, J., Greenstadt, R., Litwack, P., Tibetts, R.: Covert messaging through TCP timestamps. In: International Workshop on Privacy Enhancing Technologies (2002)
11. Sabeti, V., Shoaei, M.: New high secure network steganography method based on packet length. ISC Int. J. Inf. Secur. **12**(1), 24–44 (2020)
12. Bedi, P., Dua, A.: ARPNetSteg: network steganography using address resolution protocol. Int. J. Electron. Telecommun. **66**(4), 671–677 (2020)
13. Dua, A., Jindal, V., Bedi, P.: Covert communication using address resolution protocol broadcast request messages. In: 2021 9th International Conference on Reliability, Infocom Technologies and Optimization (Trends and Future Directions) (ICRITO), pp. 1–6. IEEE (2021)
14. Ray B., Mishra S.: Secure and reliable covert channel. In: 4th Annual Workshop on Cyber Security and Information Intelligence Research: Developing Strategies to Meet the Cyber Security and Information Intelligence (2008)
15. Bedi, P., Dua, A.: Network steganography using extension headers in IPv6. In: Badica, C., Liatsis, P., Kharb, L., Chahal, D. (eds.) ICICCT 2020. CCIS, vol. 1170, pp. 98–110. Springer, Singapore (2020). https://doi.org/10.1007/978-981-15-9671-1_8
16. Lewandowski, G., Lucena, N.B., Chapin, S.J.: Analyzing network-aware active wardens in IPv6. In: Camenisch, J.L., Collberg, C.S., Johnson, N.F., Sallee, P. (eds.) IH 2006. LNCS, vol. 4437, pp. 58–77. Springer, Heidelberg (2007). https://doi.org/10.1007/978-3-540-74124-4_5
17. Caviglione, L., Mazurczyk, W., Zuppelli, M., Schaffhauser, A., Repetto, M.: Kernel-level tracing for detecting stegomalware and covert channels in Linux environments. Comput. Netw. **191**, 108010 (2021)
18. Repetto, M., Caviglione, L., Zuppelli, M.: bccstego: a framework for investigating network covert channels. In: The 16th International Conference on Availability, Reliability and Security, pp. 1–7 (2021)
19. Abdulrahman, S., Ma, X. Peytchev, E.: Detection and classification of covert channels in IPv6 using enhanced machine learning. In: Proceedings of International Conference on Computer Technology and Information Systems (2015)
20. Senaid A., Rashid F.: A deep learning-based approach to detect covert channels attacks and anomaly in new generation internet protocol IPv6. Master's thesis (2020)
21. Wireshark. https://www.wireshark.org. Accessed 29 Dec 2021

Evolutionary Computing through Machine Learning

Image Caption Generation for Low Light Images

Navyadhara Gogineni[(✉)], Yashashvini Rachamallu, Rineeth Saladi,
and K. V. V. Bhanu Prakash

Department of Computer Science and Engineering, PES University, Bengaluru, India
navyadhara79@gmail.com

Abstract. Image captioning is the task of understanding an image and generating semantically and grammatically correct text captions. Existing work on image caption generation is mainly done on images set in optimal conditions, i.e., bright light conditions. This paper focuses on generating image captions for twilight/low-light images. The photos are processed through a Retinex theory-based enhancement algorithm to enhance the details of low-light images. A deep learning model with encoder-decoder architecture is implemented and trained with the Flickr 8k dataset for generating captions for improved photos. The efficiency of the caption generator is verified using the BLEU score, an available metric for evaluating machine-translated text.

Keywords: Image enhancement · Retinex based methods · Deep learning · Encoder-decoder architecture · Object detection · Illumination map · RNN · CNN · LSTM · Embeddings · Transformer · BLEU

1 Introduction

Caption generation came a long way from once being considered impossible by a computer to being one of the significant developments in modern technology. The development of deep learning and the open availability of extensive data caused caption generation to emerge as one of the leading areas of research. Most recent developments in Image captioning have set up research in optimal situations like having images in a decent brightness. Caption generation for low-light images is one of the challenging deep learning problems, which generates the human-readable sentence for the given low light Image.

Image enhancement helps in improving the quality and increases the understandable content of the Image and allows most applications to achieve good results for further implementations. In addition, image enhancement sharpens the Image and helps identify the required details of the Image.

Caption Generation helps summarize the Image, i.e., converting the Image to a semantically correct sentence and relatable to the Image. This requires understanding the Image and the language model for generating the captions. This task is far more complex than object detection because we have to make sure that the generated sentence is relatable to the given input image.

C. Badica et al. (Eds.): ICICCT 2022, CCIS 1670, pp. 57–72, 2022.
https://doi.org/10.1007/978-3-031-20977-2_5

Low light scenarios are hard to read. Even for humans with good eyesight, most objects go unseen due to a lack of reflecting light, and the whole scene becomes incomprehensible. Some people suffer from medical conditions like night blindness, making it even more challenging to see and understand a low-light scene. It is where having a system that generates human-readable text captions for images is most helpful. The importance of having a captioning system for low light images is not limited to medical reasons but can be significant in many real-life situations.

The primary application of caption generation is to help visually impaired people. It can also be used in content retrievals, helps in image indexing, and helps in the medical field, and social media. This can also be used for photo editing recommendations.

Here, we are working on the Flickr 8K dataset, which has a collection of 8000 images. In this paper, we reviewed the implementation of our applications, their use cases, the restrictions on data, and the system requirements.

2   Related Work

2.1   Image Enhancement

Image enhancement is a beneficial process for multiple reasons. Image enhancement helps in improving the quality and increases the understandable content of the Image. i.e., sharpening the image and helping identify the required details of the Image. Many available image enhancement methods are explained in these papers [1–3]. This paper [9] proposed the dataset that has been used to test image enhancement. Some of the methods that can be used for image enhancement are:

1. **Gray transformation methods:** The gray transformation principle is to change the grey value into another value. Gray transformation methods are divided into two categories:

   1) Linear Transformation
   2) Nonlinear Transformation

2. **Histogram equalization methods:** If the image's pixel values are evenly spread throughout all conceivable grey levels, the image has strong contrast and a wide dynamic range. It employs the cumulative distribution function. We may then arrange the output to be uniformly distributed, allowing buried features in dark areas to reappear.

3. **Methods based on image fusion:** These photos were captured simultaneously with various sensors or at different times with the same sensor. We can get a better image by combining the valuable bits of several photos. In image fusion, there are two sub-methods:

   1) Multispectral image fusion
   2) Image fusion based on background highlighting
   3) Fusion based on multiple exposures

4. **Fusion based on defogging methods:** When an RGB image is obtained in low light, the visual impression is inverted, similar to a daytime photograph captured in a foggy environment. We can improve the image by defogging and flipping it again.
5. **Retinex Based Methods**

2.2 Object Detection

Object detection can be used to identify the objects present in the Image. These papers [4, 10] helped us understand the available object detection methods and helped us choose the proper method for our scenario. From these papers, we understood that object detection could have multiple uses, and one such use case is to act as a testing criterion for image enhancement.

2.3 Caption Generation

Caption Generation helps summarize the Image, i.e., generates a semantically and grammatically correct summary of the Image in the form of a sentence. This requires understanding the Image and the language model for generating the captions. These papers [5–8] have helped us understand various methods of Image captioning feasible and helped us conclude a method suitable for our scenario. This task is far more challenging than object detection because we have to make sure that the generated sentence is relatable to the given input image.

From the research there are two methods to perform image captioning:

- **Traditional ML methods** which include SIFT, HOG, LBP. The extracted features are then passed into a classifier like SVM for classification.
- **Deep learning methods use** deep learning methods. Ex: CNN's, which learn the features of the images followed by RNN for image caption generation.

There were many possible methods to achieve this task, but only a few would fit the problem posed. These papers explained what methods and metrics could generate text captions for images. The survey papers have also helped choose proper metrics for evaluating text captions.

3 Dataset

We have worked with two datasets, one for image enhancement and another for Image captioning itself. The ExDark Dataset [9] has above 7000 low-light images, which have images ranging from meager light to low light scale for 12 distinct object classes annotated. We worked with low-light photos, i.e., images shot under twilight conditions that are barely visible to the naked eye during night times. Sample images are given in Fig. 1.

The following formula (1) determines whether the Image is dark.

$$brightness = sqrt(.241\ R2 + .691\ G2 + .68\ B2) \tag{1}$$

Fig. 1. Sample images from the ExDark dataset

A threshold value of 90 was decided by the Trial-and-Error method. If the brightness value is less than the threshold value, we say the Image is dark.

We used the 'Flickr 8k' dataset consisting of around 8,000 pictures. There are about 40,000 captions/descriptions where each Image is paired with five different captions with clear descriptions corresponding to the Image for training and testing our Image captioning model. Images and images with corresponding descriptions are given in Fig. 2 and Fig. 3, respectively.

Fig. 2. Sample Flickr8k images   **Fig. 3.** Sample Flickr8k captions

4   Proposed Solution and Architecture

This paper proposes the solution to Image captioning for low light images, which is built upon two things as in Fig. 4:

1. Image enhancement of low light images using Retinex-based methods.

2. Caption Generator using Attention Encoder-Decoder Model.

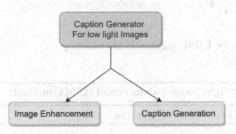

Fig. 4. Components of System

4.1 Image Enhancement Architecture

To improve the Image, we employed a Retinex-based approach called LIME. As said, Retinex Based methods are used to enhance the Image. Retinex Theory says Image is the product of illumination and reflectance of the object, i.e., **L= R.T..**, where L is the Original Image, R is Expected Output Image (Enhanced Image), and T is the Illumination Map.

4.1.1 Image Pre-processing

The input image given by the user is taken, and further improvement of the Image, i.e., suppressing the unwanted details and enhancing the required features, which helps in further implementation.

4.1.2 Image Enhancement

The processed Image is taken as input and enhances the Image, i.e., increasing the interpretability and understanding of the Image using Retinex-based methods. The Retinex Based approach is based on the human understanding of color and color invariance modeling. It uses a nonlinear spatial/spectral transform to combine heavy local contrast enhancement with color consistency. The significant advantage of this method is that it is fast and easy to implement. Here, we are implementing the LIME, i.e., Low light Image enhancement using Illumination Map Estimation.

4.1.3 Denoising of Enhanced Image

This helps remove noise from the enhanced noisy Image to restore the true Image (This step is optional depending on the enhanced Image), and you would be outputted with the enhanced Image (Fig. 5).

Fig. 5. Image enhancement architecture

The algorithm for the LIME method is as below:

Algorithm: Low light image enhancement (LIME method) Input:

Lowlight Image L, Coefficient l, gamma factor γ

1. Estimate the initial illumination map T_hat of L (Low light image)
2. Refine illumination map T based on T_hat using a sped-up solver
3. Perform a gamma correction of T using gamma factor
4. Enhance the low light image L using $\mathbf{L = R \cdot T}$
5. Perform denoising using BM3D and recompose the image.

Output: Enhanced Image

4.2 Data and Text Preprocessing

Some preprocessing functions are defined to process the raw input Images and descriptions into the proper required format. First, a pre-trained Convolutional Neural Network, EfficientNetB0, is used to encode and extract the features of the input image. An LSTM-based Recurrent Neural Network (or) RNN with an attention layer as a decoder to convert the features to sentences; Beam Search to decipher a caption with the highest likelihood.

Input data consists of images and captions describing the corresponding Image. We need the process both the images into a felicitous format for the CNN network and the text captions into the proper format for the RNN network. According to the pretrained model, Images are resized to (299,299,3).

With the use of the NLTK library, various preprocessing steps were implemented. They include:

1. Removing stop words
2. Removing punctuations
3. Utilizing regex to remove single characters.
4. Tokenization of sentences.
5. Addition of <start>, <end> tokens

The processed text is converted into embeddings with the help of the Text Vectorization technique. The TextVectorization layer is used to process the text, which is in the string to integer sequences in which the integer denotes the index of the word. A special standardization like removing < and > is used. White spaces are also taken care of.

4.3 Caption Generator Architecture

We adopted attention-based encoder-decoder architecture for the caption generator. This is because attention-based architecture has a definite advantage over sequential or attention-less architecture in carefully choosing the semantics and syntax.

4.3.1 Convolutional Neural Networks

CNNs extract features from images; an encoder helps extract the image features, which can be fed further to the RNN. Here, CNN extracts the features instead of classification, which is achieved by removing the last layer in the CNN.

→ EfficientNetB0 : Input Size : (299, 299, 3); Output Size : (None, 100, 1280)

4.3.2 Recurrent Neural Networks and LSTM

Recurrent neural nets are artificial neural networks in which the connections between the units form a directed cycle. The advantage of employing RNN over a traditional feed-forward net is that it can process an arbitrary set of inputs using its memory. For a better understanding of RNN, refer to Fig. 6

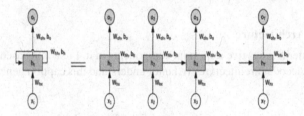

Fig. 6. Simple RNN representation

Recurrent Networks consist of several copies of the same network, each sending a message to the next. One of the issues with the RNNs is that they do not account for long-term interdependence. For example, "I grew up in England, I speak fluent English," If a NN is attempting to predict the last word, i.e., English in the phrase, it must first understand that the language name followed by the fluent is reliant on the context of the term England. Required data and the point where it's needed may grow too wide, in which case traditional RNNs will fail. To overcome this problem, LSTMs have been introduced. LSTM, like traditional RNNs, has a chain-like structure. However, the repeating modules in an LSTM network have a distinct structure. Figure 7 depicts the simple LSTM network

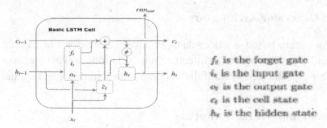

Fig. 7. Simple LSTM neural network

The cell state in the LSTM acts as the long-term memory, which helps the LSTM to keep track of the previous data. In the case of LSTM processing, the input sequence is one word at a time, which implies it cannot do the computation for timestep t until the computation for time-step t-1 is finished. Training and inference are slowed as a result of this. To overcome this issue, we used Transformers. They do parallel processing on all the words in the sequence, considerably speeding up computing. It makes no difference how far apart the words are in the input sequence. It can compute relationships between words that are close together and far apart ones. To focus on certain parts of the input sentence while predicting the output, we used attention layers and positional embeddings, which help in increasing the accuracy metrics. Positional Embeddings make Encoder perform better on less training data.

4.3.3 Model Architecture

The caption generator has five important components in it. First, it is based on attention-based encoder-decoder architecture. To better understand this caption generation model, refer to Fig. 8.

1. *CNN*: It is used to extract the features of the Image. In this application, we used EfficientNetB0 pre-trained on imagenet.
2. *Transformer Encoder*: The extracted features are then transferred to a transformer-based encoder, transforming the inputs into a new representation. The encoder sends its data to a multi-head self-attention layer here. Finally, the feed-forward layer receives the attention output and transmits it to the decoder.
3. *Transformer Decoder*: The structure of a decoder is similar to that of an encoder, with a few exceptions. It attempts to learn how to generate the caption using the encoder output and the text data sequence as inputs. Here, the decoder sends its data to the multi-head self-attention layer. This functions in a somewhat different manner than the encoder. Only earlier spots in the sequence are allowed to be attended to. Upcoming hiding positions accomplish this. The Decoder, unlike the Encoder, features a second multi-head attention layer, referred to as the Encoder-Decoder attention layer. The Encoder-Decoder attention layer is similar to Selfattention, except it takes two sources of input: the Self-attention layer below it and the Encoder stack output. The Self-attention output is passed into a Feed-forward layer, sending its output upwards to the next Decoder.

4. *Attention*: The attention mechanism aids in focusing on the most critical aspects of a sentence while ignoring the less critical aspects. Attention is employed in two places in the transformer decoder:

    a. Self-attention: The decoder's input is supplied to all three parameters, Query, Key, and Value.
    b. Encoder-Decoder Attention: The absolute encoder output is supplied to the value and critical parameters. As the query parameter, we passed the output of the self-attention modules below.

5. *Sentence Generator:* It contains linear layers. The Decoder vector is projected into Word Scores by the Linear layer, which assigns a score value to each unique word in the target vocabulary at each point in the sentence. The score values represent the probability of each word in the vocabulary appearing in that location of the sentence. After that, the Softmax layer converts the scores into possibilities. Next, we identify the index for the highest-probability word in each position and then map that index to the relevant word in the lexicon. The Transformer's output sequence is made up of those words.

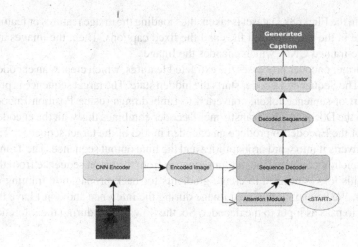

Fig. 8. Caption generator architecture

The integrated architecture of the whole Image captioning for low light images is described in Fig. 9

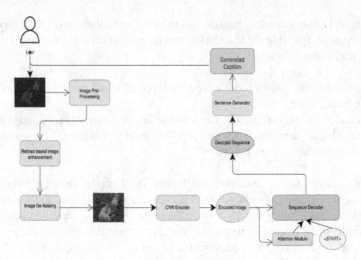

Fig. 9. System architecture

5 Training of Caption Generator

A data batch from the Flickr 8k Dataset is taken, thus loading the image features or feature vectors available in the preprocessed files and the fixed captions. Then, the images are passed to the pre-trained CNN, which encodes the Image.

The Transformer encoder processes the extracted features, which creates an encoded representation. The Sequence Decoder starts the hidden state. The target sequence is pre-fixed with a start-of-sentence token, converted to Embeddings (using Position Encoding), and sent to the Decoder. The Transformer Decoder combines this with the encoded representation of the Encoder to produce an encoded model of the target sequence. The Output layer converts it into word probabilities and the final output sequence. The Transformer's Loss function compares the output sequence from the target sequence from the training data. This loss is utilized to create gradients for back-propagation training of the Transformer. We have only the input image during the inference and don't have the target sequence to pass as input to the decoder. So, the flow of data during the inference is as follows.

1. The input image is sent through the CNN and extracts the features.
2. The extracted features are sent through the Transformer encoder and produce an encoded representation.
3. We utilize an empty sequence with simply a start-of-sentence token instead of the target sequence. This is then transformed into Embeddings (with Position Encoding) and supplied to the Decoder.
4. The Decoder combines this with the encoded representation of the Encoder to produce an encoded model of the target sequence.
5. The output layer transforms the data into word probabilities and generates a sequence of outputs.
6. The predicted word is the last in the output sequence.

7. Our Decoder input sequence has a start-of-sentence token and the first word in the second slot.
8. Return to step #3. Feed the new Decoder sequence into the model as previously. After that, append the second word of the output to the Decoder sequence. Repeat until an end-of-sentence token is predicted. We don't have to repeat steps #1 and #2 because the Encoder sequence doesn't vary on each iteration.

Loss Function: During training, we compare the generated output probability distribution to the goal sequence using a loss function such as cross-entropy loss.

6 Experimentation

6.1 Testing Procedure

6.1.1 Image Enhancement

The tests for the image enhancement algorithm have been done on the ExDark dataset, and the results were awe-inspiring. Below are some samples (Fig. 10).

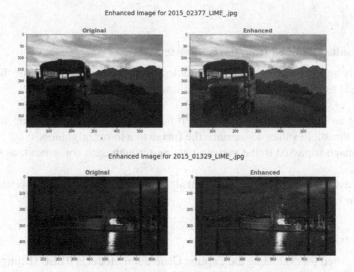

Fig. 10. Results obtained by image enhancement algorithm

6.1.2 Object Detection

Object detection acts as a test criterion for how well the details in the low light images have been enhanced. The results show that the image enhancement algorithm enriches the details well enough for detection (Fig. 11).

Fig. 11. Results obtained by object detection model

6.1.3 Results Obtained from the Complete System

This test is an integration of all the modules in the system. The flow of the testing procedure is as in Fig. 9. The procedure followed is as below:

1. Taking an image from a web/dataset, if the Image's brightness is more significant than a threshold value, de-enhance the Image to a lower brightness.
2. The Image is passed to the system, passing through each component, as shown in Fig. 9.
3. First passing through the enhancement algorithm, the enhanced Image is later passed into the captioning model.

6.1.4 Metrics

The metric used for evaluating the Caption Generation Model is BLEU (Bilingual Evaluation Understudy Score). The BLEU score is between 0 and 1, indicating how well the predicted texts resemble the reference sentences.

The Bleu Score has following variations:

- The unigram Precision score is used by BLEU-1.
- The geometric average of unigram and bigram precision is used by BLEU-2.
- BLEU-3 employs the geometric average of unigram, bigram, and trigram precision, among other things.
- BLEU-4 uses the geometric average of unigram, bigram, and trigram and multi-gram precision.

BLEU score can be calculated as: [11]

$$\log \text{BLEU} = \min(1 - \frac{r}{c}, 0) + \sum_{n=1}^{N} w_n \log p_n.$$

P_n = Modified N-gram precision
W_n = Positive weights
c = Length of candidate translation
r = Effective corpus length
Advantages of BLEU:

- BLEU is simple to compute and comprehend.
- BLEU is similar to how a human would analyze the same content.
- BLEU is also language-independent, making it simple to incorporate into your NLP models.
- When you have more than one ground truth sentence, you can use BLEU.
- Finally, it's widely used, making it easier to compare your results to other people's work.

The results obtained from the system are very impressive. Unfortunately, few results are displayed in Table 1.

Table 1. A table containing results obtained from the whole system

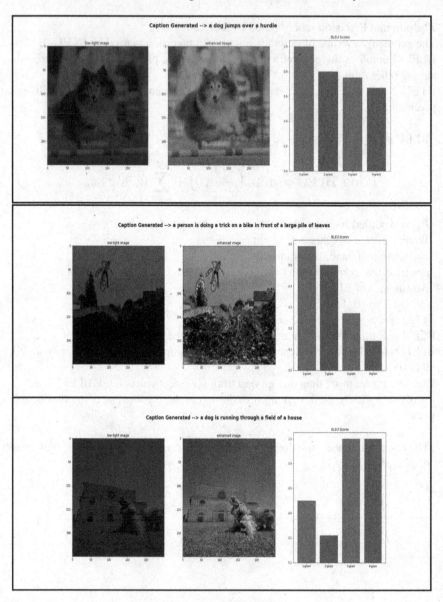

7 Use Cases

Image captioning for low-light images has a wide variety of applications. Some of them are:

1. It can be used to help people having vision problems in dark situations.

2. Content Retrieval and image indexing.
3. Social media organizations can use it to caption dark images and produce recommendations based on the Image context.
4. Usage in virtual assistants.
5. Lots of NLP-related applications.

8 Future Works

In the real world, it's hard to collect data containing images and corresponding captions. Generating image captions without any paired data is one of the challenging and limited works available. In the future, we can try to generate captions for low-light images without any paired captions in an unsupervised manner. We can also try increasing the speed of Image enhancement by processing the Image.

9 Conclusion

In this paper, we propose a new system that generates text captions for images taken in low light/twilight conditions with the help of a Retinex-based image enhancement algorithm for image enhancement and attention-based encoder-decoder architecture for text caption generation. BLEU score has been used to validate the generated captions. The system produced captions that are semantically and syntactically correct and relatable to the input image taken under low light.

The limitation of the system is that the image enhancement algorithm over sharpens the low-light image in some cases and can be improved.

References

1. Wang, W., Wu, X., Yuan, X., Gao, Z.: An experiment-based review of low-light image enhancement methods. IEEE Access **8**, 87884–87917 (2020). https://doi.org/10.1109/ACCESS.2020.2992749
2. Gu, Z., Chen, C., Zhang, D.-Y.: A low-light image enhancement method based on image degradation model and pure pixel ratio prior. Math. Probl. Eng. **2018**, 1–19 (2018). https://doi.org/10.1155/2018/8178109
3. Fu, X., Zeng, D., Huang, Y., Liao, Y., Ding, X., Paisley, J.W.: A fusion-based enhancing method for weakly illuminated images. Signal Process. **129**, 82–96 (2016)
4. Wu, X., Sahoo, D., Hoi, S.C.H.: Recent advances in deep learning for object detection. Neurocomputing **396**, 39–64 (2020)
5. Feng, Y., Ma, L., Liu, W., Luo, J.: Unsupervised image captioning. In: 2019 IEEE/CVF Conference on Computer Vision and Pattern Recognition (CVPR), p. 41204129 (2019). https://doi.org/10.1109/CVPR.2019.00425
6. Hossain, M.Z., Sohel, F., Shiratuddin, M.F., Laga, H.: A comprehensive survey of deep learning for image captioning. ACM Comput. Surv. **51**, 1–36 (2019)
7. Vinyals, O., Toshev, A., Bengio, S., Erhan, D.: Show and tell: a neural image caption generator. In: 2015 IEEE Conference on Computer Vision and Pattern Recognition (CVPR), pp. 3156–3164 (2015)

8. Sandeep, N.P., Sukhendu, D.: A Bottom-Up and Top-Down Approach for Image Captioning using Transformer, pp. 1–9 (2018). https://doi.org/10.1145/3293353.3293391
9. Loh, Y.P., Chan, C.S.: Getting to know low-light images with the exclusively dark dataset. Comput. Vis. Image Understand. **178**, 30–42 (2019). https://doi.org/10.1016/j.cviu.2018.10.010
10. Guo, H., Lu, T., Wu, Y.: Dynamic low-light image enhancement for object detection via end-to-end training. In: 2020 25th International Conference on Pattern Recognition (ICPR), pp. 5611–5618 (2021). https://doi.org/10.1109/ICPR48806.2021.9412802
11. Papineni, K., Roukos, S., Ward, T., Zhu, W.: Bleu: a method for automatic evaluation of machine translation. ACL (2002)

A Study on Feature Selection for Gender Detection in Speech Processing for Assamese Language

Kankana Dutta(✉) ⓘ, Rizwan Rehman, Priyakshi Mahanta, and Ankumon Sarmah

Centre For Computer Science and Applications, Dibrugarh University, Dibrugarh, India
{kankanadutta,rizwan,priyakshimahanta,ankumonsarmah}@dibru.ac.in

Abstract. Gender identification is an integral part of a Speech recognition system. Specifically, for the low resource languages, it is a challenging task. For any speech recognition system, finding a suitable feature plays an essential role in the system's performance. In this paper, we have done a comparative analysis of gender identification from formant frequencies F1 and F2 of speech data set collected from the speakers of Assamese language (a low recourse language of North-East India). The objective is to explore different classification techniques for developing a gender identification module for Assamese language. We have used four supervised classification techniques kNN, Logistic Regression, decision tree, and SVM, and found that when F1 and F2 are used together, the methods give the best result. One unsupervised method Gaussian Mixture Model (GMM) is also applied and found that the best result is given by formant frequency F1.

Keywords: Gender identification · Speech processing system · Formant frequency · Supervised learning method · Un-supervised learning method

1 Introduction

Speech processing-related research has gained much attention in the last few decades. Also, people nowadays prefer to use speech recognition systems which are helpful in many ways. A speech signal is an acoustic wave that can provide different information related to the speaker and the language being spoken. The information regarding the speaker may include age, gender, speaker identity, the emotional status of the speaker, and many more. Different parameters or features are collected from the speech signal, and different methods are applied to find the required information. These features collected from speech signals are fundamental frequency, also referred to as pitch and format frequencies. Formant frequency refers to the resonance frequencies of the vocal tract. The different types of formant frequencies are F1, F2, F3, and F4. Vowel formant frequencies are the most used voice features in the field of speech processing research. Mel Frequency Cepstral Coefficients (MFCC), Linear Prediction Coefficients (LPC), Linear Prediction Cepstral Coefficients (LPCC), Line Spectral Frequencies (LSF), Discrete Wavelet Transform (DWT), and Perceptual Linear Prediction (PLP) are other speech

C. Badica et al. (Eds.): ICICCT 2022, CCIS 1670, pp. 73–82, 2022.
https://doi.org/10.1007/978-3-031-20977-2_6

feature extraction techniques which are also used widely in the field of speech processing to extract information or features from the speech signal. Identifying the most salient features and analyzing and finding the desired information from a large set of data is a challenging task. Different machine learning techniques, which help analyze a large set of data, maybe applied and construct a classification model for a particular task.

Assamese language speaker is found mainly in Assam, which is a state in India, and more than 15 million people speak this language. Assam is a state of multi-lingual and multi-ethnic people. Apart from the Assamese language, tribal language speakers such as Bodo, Mising, Rabha, Karbi, and Dimasa are found in different districts of Assam. Other languages like Nepali, Hindi, etc. are also spoken by a large number of the population which are spread all over the state. In the last few years, some researchers have been working in the field of speech processing and trying to develop different applications for Assamese as well as other regional languages spoken in Assam.

Gender Identification is a part of a speech recognition system that finds the gender of a speaker from the speech information extracted from the speech signal. The information about gender can be helpful in speaker recognition systems which are used in different security systems today.

1.1 Literature Review

This review covers the work related to speech processing research done for Assamese and other tribal languages of Assam and some recent works done for other languages.

Talukdar et al. [1] analyzed Cepstral features and formant frequencies of Bodo and Rabha phonemes and words using LPC and observed that Cepstral coefficients of Bodo and Rabha vowels had shown distinctive characteristics for male and female speakers. The variation of the cepstral coefficients for males is very irregular, and the same for the female is stable.

An automatic Language Identification (LID) system was developed for the languages Bodo, Dimasa, Rabha, and Tiwa, which belong to the same language subfamily, and identifies the language from a short sound file [2]. The system was implemented using a Gaussian mixture model with Mel-Frequency Cepstral Coefficients (MFCCs) as features and showed 92.7% accuracy when the duration of the speech file is 3 s.

An automatic Assamese vowel recognition system from spoken Assamese words [3] was developed by P Sharma *et al.* using Support Vector Machine (SVM), K-Nearest Neighbor (kNN), and Random Forest (RF) classifier and found that Random Forest provides better recognition rate than other two classifiers.

Mridusmita Sharma and Kandarpa Kumar Sarma [4] used Recurrent Neural Network (RNN) based algorithm and k-Nearest Neighbor (kNN) based algorithm for the recognition of the vowels of the Assamese language for four major dialects of the language. The kNN based approach gave a better recognition rate than ANN.

A study on Missing language vowels was performed by Rehman R. *et al.* using the Fisher score algorithm [5] to find the most distinctive feature of speech data for gender classification. The result is cross-validated with a Tree-based algorithm and found that fundamental formant frequencies (F0) are the best parameter among all the other parameters.

A study on different attributes of speech signals like time, pitch, formant frequencies, and speaker type was done on Missing language vowels by Saikia U. *et al.* in 2019 [6] using a regression model and found that fundamental formant frequencies (F0), i.e. pitch, varies for the vowels with the gender of the speaker and this information can be utilized for speaker identification in Mising language. A logistic regression model is built and applied on pitch value (F0) to detect the gender of the speaker [7] and can detect the gender.

An automatic transcription model of the Assamese language [8] was developed by Sarma, H., *et al.* to represent the speech sound with a symbol which is known as phonetic transcription. The experiment was done using Hidden Markov Mode Tool Kit (HTK).

Sarma H. *et al.* worked on different aspects of speech-to-text processing using HTK [9] and developed an automatic syllabification model for the Assamese language to find the syllables of a word automatically and found 12 different syllable patterns where five are found most frequent.

An automatic speech recognition system for Assamese was implemented using Kaldi Toolkit for continuously spoken Assamese [10] by Deka *et al.,* and experiments were conducted to explore the effect of excluding low-quality speech files from the training set on the performance of the system.

Basu J, *et al.* developed a multi-lingual speech corpus for Low-Resource Eastern and North-Eastern Indian Languages for Speaker and Language Identification [11] and found the Best performance of 94.49% (using MFCC (Mel frequency cepstral coefficients) + SDC(shifted delta cepstral) feature and LSTM-RNN) in Speaker identification and 95.69% (using MFCC + SDC feature and LSTM-RNN) in Language identification for short duration speech files.

Analysis of the first three formant frequencies was presented by Dr. Bhargab Medhi using the LPC model and observed that the variation of F1and F2 for a different vowel is quite distinct, formant values of a female speaker are comparatively high than the male speaker, and the third formant frequency F3 does not play a crucial role in the identification of a specific vowel spectrum [12].

Yücesoy, E proposed a model for gender and age group classification using MFCC and delta coefficients of speech values applied in the Gaussian Mixer model [13]. A test has been carried out to find the minimum number of GMM components.

A gender recognition system was developed by Kumar P. *et al.* [14] where the front end extracted speech signal features such as energy, ZCR, MFCC, and Entropy, and the back end classified the speaker according to gender using GMM.

A speaker recognition system was developed by Gupta M. *et al.* [15], with a two-level approach where first the gender will be identified, and then the speaker is recognized. MFCC and pitch values are used for gender recognition with the SVM classifier, and MFCC, Pitch, and RASTA-PLP features are used for speaker recognition using GMM.

Alkhawaldeh R.S discusses and uses three prominent feature selection techniques EA, PSO, and wolf techniques to find the optimal features from MFCCs, Chroma, Mel, Contrast, and Tonnetz for improving the result of classification techniques [16].

1.2 Motivation and Contribution

From the literature review, it is observed that several experiments have been carried out to evaluate experiments on Gender, language, and speech identification in Assamese language and other regional languages of Assam using different classification models. It is also observed that the most used feature type extracted from the audio file was MFCC to identify the speaker. It is also used for the speech recognition process. In the case of gender recognition, mostly fundamental frequency (F0) and formant frequencies (F1–F4) of speech signals were used. Different approaches and classifiers such as SVM, KNN, RNN, Tree-based model, and Regression model were used on formant frequencies in gender recognition. The first two formants i.e. F1 and F2 show distinct features in the case of male and female speakers of the languages Assamese, Bodo, Rabha, and Mising [1, 5–7, 12].

Based on these observations, we are performing a study on Assamese speech data using different prominent classification models. The aim is to study the impact of the formant frequencies F1 and F2 in the case of gender identification. We have only considered F1 and F2 because the main information of a speech signal is concentrated in the low-frequency part of a speech signal. Thus the objective of this study can be defined as

1. To study the performance of different supervised machine learning methods on the formant frequencies F1 and F2.
2. To study the performance of these formant frequency values in the Gaussian Mixture Model (GMM), which is an unsupervised learning method, and
3. To determine which of these formant frequencies show the better result in gender identification for the Assamese language.

2 Methodology

This section describes the dataset and methods used to experiment.

2.1 Dataset

The dataset contains data from both male and female speakers. There are total 23 numbers of speakers, out of which 15 are male, and 8 are female. A speech sample from each speaker is collected speaking the Assamese vowels. In the Assamese language, there is a total of 11 vowels, and all these vowels are spoken by the speakers. There is a total of 4822 speech samples present in the dataset. The data are recorded in a noise-free environment. For the current study, we have used only two formant frequencies, F1 and F2, of the speech samples. These formant frequencies are extracted by using PRAAT software.

The features are plotted in a graph for both males and females, as shown in Fig. 1 and Fig. 2, respectively.

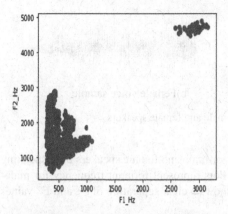

Fig. 1. F1 and F2 features for females   **Fig. 2.** F1 and F2 features for male

2.2 Methods

For analyzing the data, we are using different prominent machine learning methods. Two types of machine learning methods are used here- supervised and unsupervised methods.

In supervised learning, the machine is trained with some known data. The data used to train the model are already labelled with the correct class. The machine is trained with labelled data, and whenever some new information is obtained, it calculates the answer with the trained data. In this experiment, four prominent supervised learning methods are being used, viz., k Nearest Neighbour (kNN), Support Vector Machine (SVM), Logistic Regression, and Decision Tree method. On the other hand, in the unsupervised learning method, the data does not have any label to help in the classification method; it is designed to find the label on its own. Unsupervised methods are helpful in complex processing tasks compared to supervised methods. In this experiment, one unsupervised method is being used, Gaussian Mixture Model (GMM). GMM is a probabilistic model which represents the clusters as a weighted sum of Gaussian component densities. This GMM model is used in many experiments performed on Assamese as well as other regional languages and found that GMM shows promising results in these languages.

3 Results and Discussion

The speech spectrum contains different information about the speaker. For this study of gender recognition, only f1 and f2 formant frequencies are considered. Figure 3 shows two voice samples of male and female speakers speaking the first Assamese vowel.

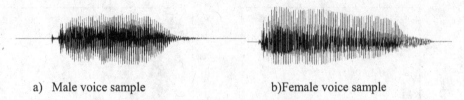

a) Male voice sample   b)Female voice sample

Fig. 3. Voice sample of male and female speakers

Figure 4 represents F1 and F2 features for male and female speakers both speaking the first Assamese vowel. Green and blue dots represent formant frequency for male-female speakers, respectively. This figure shows a clear separation of F1 and F2 values for male and female speakers.

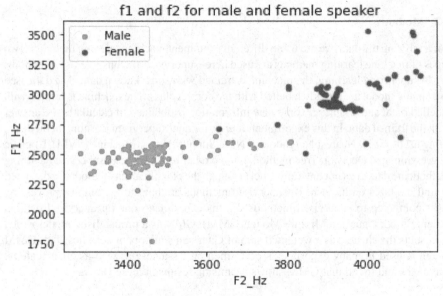

Fig. 4. F1 and F2 representation of male and female speakers

Table 1 represents some data from the dataset. It consists of formant values of F1 and F2 along with the gender.

After extracting the speech features F1 and F2 from the speech signals, KNN, Logistic Regression, SVM, and Decision Tree methods are applied to these features. These methods are supervised machine learning algorithms. Data processing is carried out using Python. First, these classification methods are applied using the formant frequency feature F1 and then using the feature F2. Also, classifiers are applied using both the features F1 and F2 together. The database is divided into 80% training data and 20% test data. Table 2 shows the experiment results.

Table 1. Some example data from the dataset

Sl. No	F1_Hz	F2_HZ .	Gender
1	904.2219	1435.993	Female
2	895.4748	1396.962	Female
3	855.5742	1386.76	Female
4	910.6128	1423.129	Female
5	884.541	1429.456	Female
6	858.5995	1441.599	Female
7	288.3647	1911.452	Male
8	277.6312	2033.321	Male
9	321.0209	1842.203	Male
10	245.2099	1963.462	Male
11	243.5955	1894.786	Male
12	367.2974	2013.839	Male

Table 2. Rate of recognition using formant frequencies

Formant frequencies	Recognition rate			
	kNN	Logistic regression	SVM	Decision tree
F1	58.34	57.36	54.25	56.59
F2	55.85	52.64	50.77	52.09
F1, F2	69.22	59.79	59.38	62.79

It is evident from the table that formant frequency F2 alone shows the worst result, and the best result is obtained by using both the formants frequencies F1 and F2 together. Among these methods, the kNN method gives the best answer when F1 and F2 are used together.

Next, we have used Gaussian Mixer Model (GMM), which is are unsupervised clustering technique. Since it is an unsupervised method, the model does not have any information about the number of clusters and data labels. Since we are classifying the data into male and female, we are applying the GMM model for creating two clusters to represent males and females. First, we have applied the model for classifying the data using the formant frequencies F1. Then we have applied the model on formant frequency F2, and finally, the model is applied using both F1 and F2 together. The graphical representation of data according to their gender plotted in a graph is shown in Fig. 5.

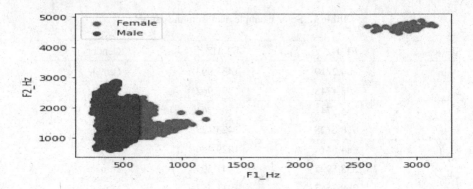

a) Using F1 feature

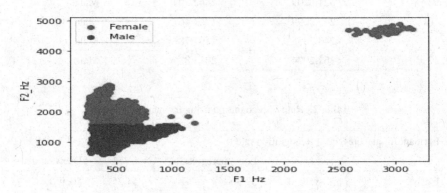

b) Using F2 feature

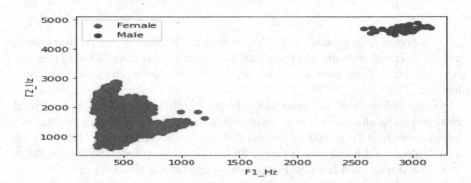

c) Using both F1 and F2

Fig. 5. (a, b, c). Clustering result by GMM

The accuracy achieved for the method is calculated for all the cases, and also precision, recall, and f1-score values are calculated and shown in Table 3.

Table 3. Error analysis of gmm method

Feature name	Precision	Recall	F1-score	Accuracy
F1	52.21	88.68	65.72	54.58%
F2	49.00	66.21	56.2	49.56%
F1, F2	0	88.68	0	50.06%

From the above results, it is seen that the model provides the best F1 score and accuracy value with the feature F1. It is ranked the attributes as F1, (F1, F2), and F3. This shows a difference in results with supervised methods where the attributes are ranked as (F1, F2), F1, and F2 according to their performance. A similar result is found in both supervised and unsupervised methods, where the F2 value gives the worst accuracy result.

4 Conclusion

In this comparative study, we have tried to find a formant frequency value between F1 and F2, which works better for gender recognition using Assamese vowels. For that, we have compared the results of supervised machine learning methods kNN, SVM, Decision Tree, and Logistic regression classifier and found that when F1 and F2 are used together, it gives the best result, and F2 gives the worst result. Again the same experiment is performed using the unsupervised method GMM and found that F1 is giving the best result. F2 is giving the worst result, which is the same in the case of supervised methods also. This experiment is done using only two formant frequency values. The accuracy rate is not very high, which suggests that these two formant frequencies are not sufficient to detect gender. More experiments can be done to find whether the performance improves when F1 and F2 are used with the other two formant frequency features, F3, F4, or with the MFCC features.

References

1. Talukdar, J., Pathak, N.: Acoustic representation of BODO and RABHA phonemes. Int. J. Comput. Commun. Network. **1**(1) (2012)
2. Chakraborty, J., Sarmah, P., Vijaya, S.: Spoken language identification of four Tibet-Burman languages, Oriental COCOSDA (2020)
3. Sarma, P., Mitra, M., Bhuyan, M.P., Deka, V., Sarmah, S., Sarma, S.K.: Automatic vowel recognition from Assamese spoken words. IJITEE **8**(10) (2019)
4. Sharma, M., Sarma, K.K.: Dialectal Assamese vowel speech detection using acoustic-phonetic features, KNN and RNN. In: 2nd International Conference on Signal Processing & Integrated Networks (2015)

5. Rehman, R., Bordoloi, K., Dutta, K., Borah, N., Mahanta, P.: Feature selection and classification of speech dataset for gender identification: a machine learning approach. J. Theoretical Appl. Inf. Technol. **99** (2020)
6. Saikia, U., Rehman, R., Hazarika, J., Hazarika, G.C.: Predictive analysis using regression methods in low resource language *"MISING"*. In: 2nd International Conference on Information Systems & Management Science (ISMS) (2019)
7. Saikia, U., Hazarika, J.: Analysis of speech signal data of Mising vowels using logistic regression and k-Means clustering. Int. J. Adv. Comput. Sci. Appl. 12(4) (2021)
8. Sarma, H., Saharia, N., Sharma, U.: Development of Assamese speech corpus and automatic transcription using HTK. Advances in Signal Processing and Intelligent Recognition Systems, Advances in Intelligent Systems and Computing (2014)
9. Sarma, H., Saharia, N., Sharma, U.: Development and analysis of speech recognition systems for Assamese language using HTK. ACM Trans. Asian Low-Resour. Lang. Inf. Process. **17**(1)(Article 7) (2017)
10. Deka, B., Sarmah, P., Vijaya, S.: Assamese database and speech recognition, IEEE (2019)
11. Basu, J., Khan, S., Roy, R., Basu, T.K., Majumder, S.: Multilingual speech corpus in low-resource eastern and northeastern indian languages for speaker and language identification. Circuits Syst. Signal Process. **40**(10), 4986–5013 (2021). https://doi.org/10.1007/s00034-021-01704-x
12. Medhi, B.: Analysis of formant frequency F1, F2, and F3 in Assamese vowel phonemes using LPC model. Int. J. Eng. Res. Technol. **6**(05) (2017)
13. Yücesoy, E.: Speaker age and gender classification using GMM super vector and NAP channel compensation method. J. Ambient Intell. Human. Comput. **13**, 3633–3642 (2020)
14. Kumar, P., Baheti, P., Jha, R.K., Sarmah, P., Sathish, K.: Voice gender detection using Gaussian Mixture Model. J. Network Commun. Emerg. Technol. **8**(4) (2018). www.jncet.org
15. Gupta, M., Bhartiy, S.S., Agarwaly, S.: Gender-Based Speaker Recognition from Speech Signals Using GMM Model. Modern Physics Letters, World Scientific Publishing Company (2019)
16. Alkhawaldeh, R.S.: DGR: Gender Recognition Of Human Speech Using One-Dimensional Conventional Neural Network. Hindawi Scientific Programming, Vol. 2019, Article ID 7213717 (2019)

Bengali Fake News Detection: Transfer Learning Based Technique with Masked LM Process by BERT

Sourav Saha[1], Aditi Sarker[2], Partha Chakraborty[2(✉)] (iD), and Mohammad Abu Yousuf[3]

[1] Department of Computer Science and Engineering, United International University, Dhaka, Bangladesh
[2] Department of Computer Science and Engineering, Comilla University, Cumilla, Bangladesh
partha.chak@cou.ac.bd
[3] Institute of Information Technology, Jahangirnagar University, Savar, Dhaka, Bangladesh
yousuf@juniv.edu

Abstract. The spread of false information is increasingly commonplace due to the internet's ease of use and people's hyperactivity on social media. Fake news spreads quickly in numerous industries such as politics, education, health, and finance, causing significant losses and having a negative impact on public life. Models centered on the Transformer infrastructure is currently showing promise in a vast scope of natural language processing tasks, featuring machine translation. So, the pre-trained deep learning-based model BERT is used in this research effort, recognizing the necessity of detecting fake news in Bangla language. Two distinct datasets used to train and test our model is publicly available. After comparing BERT model's precision, the LSTM with regularization model, the SVM model, the NB model and the CNN model with difference evaluation matrices, we inferred that our suggested BERT model outperforms them all. Our proposed model has 95% precision rate.

Keywords: BERT · Transformer · Tokenizer · Fake · Bangla

1 Introduction

Fake news has harmed numerous aspects of society, notably people being misled, politicians and public opinion being misguided, and so on. Fake news creates monetary losses in different industries such as business, stocks, and markets, therefore financial institutions have a huge challenge. Unreliable and spurious information about the COVID-19 epidemic is widely disseminated on social media, with many industrialized countries (such as the United States) claiming that the disease is spreading [1]. Speculations spreading on social media [2] have a significant jeopardize on less intelligent people, according to intelligence studies, preventing them from making the best decisions. Rumors have resulted in a number of fatalities in Bangladesh in recent days. As a result of extensive allegations about impending human sacrifices during the construction of the Padma Bridge, five people were killed and ten more were injured [3]. Anyone can share news

C. Badica et al. (Eds.): ICICCT 2022, CCIS 1670, pp. 83–96, 2022.
https://doi.org/10.1007/978-3-031-20977-2_7

swiftly due to the widening quantity of clients in web-based living. The identification of fake news based on its content is a tedious job.

The development of an efficient and effective method to detect fake news has become unavoidable. The fundamental reason for this research is the realization of the importance of avoiding the spread of fake news. We basically chose the BERT model for detecting fake news from Bengali texts because of its powerful and theoretically simple qualities in handling many natural language processing jobs. To pre-train BERT models with deep bidirectional representations from unlabeled format, provide both left and right context in all levels. BERT architecture takes a complete sentence as input and enables the model to taught word meanings from context while also making connections to other words in the text. The BERT, Masked LM (MLM) training approach is used to detect Bengali Fake new.

The remainder of the article is divided as follows: The second section evaluates pertinent work, the third segment evaluates the recommended approach, the fourth segment presents the findings and discussion, and the fifth segment provides a summary of the article.

2   Related Works

Various research methods have erupted in lately. Most research publications employ deep learning and machine learning models to provide accurate results [26–37]. To determine if a Bangla text document is a strain or not, a hybrid extraction strategy using Word2Vec, TF-IDF, and a CNN architecture-based hybrid method was applied [4]. In order to gather information from social media, comment extraction was utilized, and the results were processed using the Nave Bays classifier and TF-IDF vectorization [5]. Graph analysis was utilized to detect the origins of bogus news and map the provenance nodes [6]. [7] employed user-based functionality and node embedding to augment Twitter's appraisal of bogus news. Identifying fake news [8] introduced the notion of Social Article Fusion (SAF), that combines syntactic characteristics of headlines with community context information. Here, autoencoders represented text in two-dimensional space, while RNN recorded the user's temporal interactions with fake news. [9] employed a revolutionary blockchain-based method called Proof of Credibility (PoC) to detect and prevent bogus news. TriFN, a novel system for detecting fake news that can shield preferable connectivity from news providers, was introduced in [10], and in a research paper [11], another novel machine learning tactic that encompass news contents and social cues was introduced, and this approach was used inside the Facebook Messenger chatbot.

Nowadays, Transformer architecture-based model BERT shows processing results in the text classification task. BERT based deep learning approach was used to discern spoof news in social media. [12]. For document classification BERT model was used in [13]. To understand Arabic language BERT model was used in [14]. Based on Bidirectional Encoder Representations from Transformers (BERT) automatic fake news detection model was proposed in [15].

It clarifies that, bidirectional training technique is a top objective for modeling relevant false news information that can boost classification efficiency while seizing semantic and wide links sentences. BERT model is the best at detecting fake news, especially with a short dataset. Consequently, unlike previous models, Transformer constructs depictions of its input and outcome applying only self-attention rather than sequence-aligned RNNs or convolution. For this reason, detecting Bangla fake news transformer-based BERT model is proposed in this research work.

3   Proposed Methodology

Because of its exceptional consequences on eleven natural language processing tasks, the BERT model is primarily used in this study to detect Bangla false news. Figure 1 depicts the workflow diagram of our suggested paradigm.

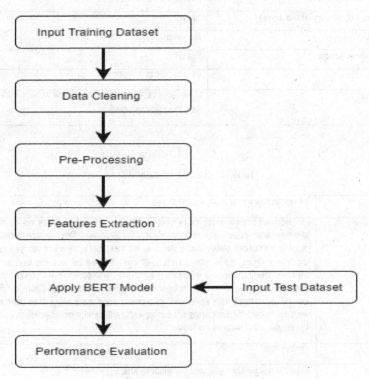

Fig. 1. Workflow diagram

At first, we take one dataset for tanning our model. Before feeding text data into the training model, it is cleaned and preprocessed to remove symbols, special characters, and numeric values. WordPiece embedding retrieves features from the data, and BERT's Masked LM processes train the model. BERT model can use existing literature on language model pre-training, and here we use Bangla BERT based pre trained language model for Bangla language. For classification, BERT pre-trained classifier is used. Then we test our model with another dataset. A variety of performance matrices are utilized to assess our model's performance.

3.1 Data Collection

For datasets initially, we are used two different datasets from train and test our model. Dataset1 retain 250 different criteria news. The sample of dataset1 [16] and dataset2 [17] are shown in Table 1 and 2 respectively.

Table 1. Sample of dataset1

ID of the news	2
(Domain)News publisher's site name	jugantor.com
Date (Published date)	2018-09-20 20:20:2
Category (Category of the news)	Sports
Source	Reporter
ad headline-article	linked
Article title	টস হেরে বোলিংয়ে বাংলাদেশ
Content	এশিয়া কাপের ষষ্ঠ ম্যাচে বাংলাদেশ দলের বিপক্ষে টস জিতে প্রথমে ব্যাট করার সিদ্ধান্ত নিয়েছেন আফগানিস্তা...

Table 2. Sample of dataset2

Title	এক দিনে করোনায় মৃত্যু ১৫ জনের, নতুন শনাক্ত ২৬৬
Statement	দেশে করোনাভাইরাসে আক্রান্ত হয়ে গত ২৪ ঘণ্টায় ১৫ জন মারা গেছেন। একই সময় দেশে করোনায় আক্রান্ত ব্যক্তি শনাক্ত হয়েছেন ২৬৬ জন। দেশে করোনায় এক দিনে মৃত্যু এই সর্বোচ্চ। এ নিয়ে দেশে করোনায় মোট মারা গেছেন ৭৫ জন। আর মোট শনাক্তের সংখ্যা ১ হাজার ৮৩৮ জন। সুস্থ হয়েছেন ৯ জন। এ নিয়ে মোট সুস্থ হলেন ৫৮ জন। ব্রিফিংয়ে বলা হয়, গত ২৪ ঘণ্টায় ২ হাজার ১৯০টি নমুনা পরীক্ষা করা হয়। এখন পর্যন্ত আক্রান্তের মধ্যে হাসপাতালে চিকিৎসা নিয়েছেন ৫০০ জনের বেশি। বাকিরা বাসায় বা কোয়ারেন্টিনে চিকিৎসা নিয়েছেন। আইসিইউ সাপোর্ট নিয়েছেন ২৭ জন। আজ বৃহস্পতিবার করোনাভাইরাস নিয়ে স্বাস্থ্য অধিদপ্তরের নিয়মিত অনলাইন ব্রিফিংয়ে এসব তথ্য জানান স্বাস্থ্যমন্ত্রী জাহিদ মালেক। গত ৮ মার্চ দেশে প্রথম করোনা আক্রান্ত ব্যক্তি শনাক্তের ঘোষণা আসে। আর গত ১৮ মার্চ করোনাভাইরাসে আক্রান্ত হয়ে প্রথম মৃত্যুর ঘটনা ঘটে। এর আগে গতকাল বৃহস্পতিবার ১০ জনের মৃত্যু হয়। আর আক্রান্ত শনাক্ত হয় ৩৪১ জনের।
Category	বাংলাদেশ সংবাদ
Source	https://www.prothomalo.com/bangladesh/article/1651410
Date	১৭ এপ্রিল ২০২০, ১৪:৪১
Class	Real

Dataset1 is primarily used to train the models, while dataset2 is utilized to test them. The summary of the datasets is depicted in Table 3 and Fig. 2 demonstrates the visualization of the data.

Table 3. The dataset's description

Dataset	Real	Fake
Dataset1	48678	1299
Dataset2	1548	993

```
0.0      3591
1.0      55880
Name: label, dtype: int64
```

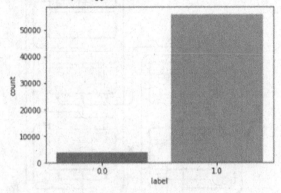

Fig. 2. Visualization of datasets

3.2 Data Selection

For training the model, we took dataset1 as input. There are "9" features are available in this dataset to build a model. Though, among them only 2 features to build the model. We took "Content" for x level and "label" for y label from the dataset.

3.3 Data Preprocessing and Features Extraction

Pre-processing is a step in the machine learning process that is utilized to adjust original data. Though this dataset contains text data it, needs to convert words into the vector to fit it in our model as input. There are several techniques had to maintain to process text data to fit in NLP-based machine learning algorithms. Techniques are Data cleaning, Tokenization, Text to sequences, Padding sequences. For tokenizing data, two techniques are used here. We applied WordPiece tokenization. It was used to train BERT model to tokenize sentences. Tokenization comes in handy when dealing with words that aren't part of one's vocabulary. After configuring our dataset and implementation publicly distributed by HuggingFace's Transformers [18] for tokenization, we used a high-optimized tokenize transformer library-based pertained model for the Bangla language.

3.4 Transformer Architecture

The transformer is a natural language processing architecture that grows with model size and training data [19]. Transformer is a library intended to enabling Transformer-based infrastructures such as BERT and making pre-trained models more widely available. Figure 3 depicts the transformer's infrastructure.

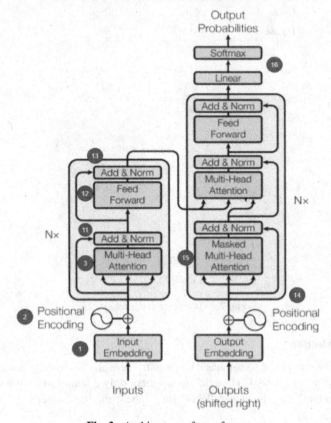

Fig. 3. Architecture of transformer

The transformer is composed of two components: encoding and decoding. Because the computer does not understand any language, the input text data is converted to vector form and a vocabulary dictionary is created. Following that, each word is assigned a numeric index. Only those words that occur in the current input text are extracted. The input is then forwarded to the embedding layer. Attached to each of the index's vectors. Each of these vectors is initially filled with random numbers. The transformer's original embedding size is 512.The importance of the word embedding is that it numerically conveys semantic meaning. Each dimension of the word embedding attempts to capture some of the word's linguistic characteristics. This may assist in determining whether this term refers to an entity or something else. If two words share similar linguistic characteristics and occur in a similar context, their data embedding values will become increasingly similar during the training process.

One of the transformer's most distinguishing characteristics is that it takes on the entire embedding at once and processes it in parallel. As a result, the transformer model performs faster than other models, but at the cost of losing critical ordering information. To address this issue, position Embedding is used to recover position data. This section introduces a new class of vectors that contain position information. By combining word embedding and position embedding, a new order of word embedding is created. Frequency is used to capture positional information, which aids in differentiating different meanings. In Eqs. 1 and 2, the sine and cosine functions that are used to generate embedding are depicted.

$$PE_{(pos,2i)} = \sin(\frac{pos}{1000^{\frac{2i}{a}}}) \tag{1}$$

$$PE_{(pos,2i+1)} = \cos(\frac{pos}{1000^{\frac{2i}{a}}}) \tag{2}$$

where pos connotes the position embedding, numbered connotes the length of the position embedding, and I connotes the index of each dimension of the position embedding. The transformer's attention mechanism assists the model in focusing on the critical word in a given sentence. It is composed of three linear layers, each of which contains a branch of simple fully connected neurons that lacks an activation function. They are primarily used to map inputs to outputs and to change the dimensions of the inputs themselves. To jointly attach data from various representation sub-locations at various positions Attention is divided into multiple heads. Each liner layer contains three distinct functions: Query, Key, and Value. The liner layer mass is enhanced by the embedding layer weights. The calculation is as follows:

$$MultiHead(Q, K, V) = Concat(head_1_____head_h)w^0 \tag{3}$$

where, $head_i = Attention(QM_i^Q, KM_i^K, VM_i^V)$. After the multiplication query, key and value matrices are generated. A score matrix is used to count how much a word has to attend to every other word. SoftMax is another score matrix that turns attention scores into the probabilities. Which helps the model to be determined on which words to attend. The output of QK and V then inject Linear layer. Encoding layer's output is poured into decoding stratum. At the first mask, multi-headed attention is done into the output and then fed into the next attention layer. To ensure the transparency of the network into the words masked multi-headed attention is essential. The model with transformer is used in our research is directed in Fig. 4:

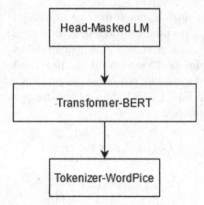

Fig. 4. Model design for our research work

3.5 Model Deployment

A pre-trained BERT library is used to build the model. Transformer bidirectional training is largely used in Bidirectional Encoder Representations from Transformer (BERT). In order to pre-train deep bidirectional structures from unmarked text, BERT plans to condition either left or right aspect at all stages. A transformer in BERT's attention mechanism learns word-to-word contextual relationships.

BERT is divided into two sections, one for encoding and the other for decoding. Text data is read via encoding, and predictions are made through decoding. We used masked LM (MLM), where words are replaced by a mask before sending to BERT. The last hidden vectors accompanying to the mask tokens inject output SoftMax of transformer. 15 percent of the tokens in each sequence are masked in this experiment.

On top of the encoding layer, the classification layer is applied. In this classification layer, the Adam optimizer is utilized, and binary cross entropy is used to evaluate the loss function. To determine the appropriate learning rate, the ktrain library is employed (Fig. 5).

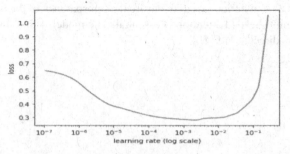

Fig. 5. Learning rate

The model is then trained using the weight, learning rate, and epoch 5 parameters that were previously set. The model dataset2 is then utilized for testing. We use four other models in addition to our proposed one: Convolutional Neutral Network (CNN), Long Short-Term Memory (LSTM), Support Vector Machine (SVM), and Nave Bayes.

CNN: Convolutional networks have been found to be excellent at classifying both short and long texts in a variety of situations [20–21]. As a result, we try to categorize bogus news using a CNN model that is similar to [20]. We employ ReLU as the network's activation function.

LSTM: One of the most extensively utilized models in text categorization and generation issues is the Long Short-Term Memory (LSTM) [22–23] network. Bidirectional LSTM (Bi-LSTM) in particular has demonstrated outstanding ability in catching sequential information from both directions in texts. The attention mechanism has also been demonstrated to be an effective pooling technique for classification issues when paired with Bi-LSTM. Here, the author investigates a Bi-LSTM model with attention at the top, which is similar to [24]. We use a total of 256 LSTM units. In the network, we use two layers of Bi-LSTM. Drop out used in LSTM and CNN model is 0.25 to avoid over fitting.

SVM and NB: The Nave Bayes classifier is a basic classification algorithm that is built on the Bayes theorem. It's hard to choose which Nave Bayes algorithm to use. They outperform Bernoulli and Gaussian Nave Bayes in text classification. Multinomial Many problems involving phrase categorization employ Nave Bayes. The support vector machine is used to solve regression or designation aspects. A text dataset is resistant to over-fitting in high-dimensional space. Given that most texts are linearly separable, the linear kernel is chosen. Similar to [17], we use SVM and MNB in this paper.

BERT [25], have recently made significant progress in a diversity of NLP tasks. We devoted the multilingual BERT model to categorize fake and true news to assess the breadth of such a language model in our work. HuggingFace's Transformers has openly provided pre-trained model weights and implementation.

4 Experimental Results and Discussion

After training, the BERT model, LSTM with regularization model and CNN model with dataset1 and testing with dataset2, different evaluation matrices are adhered to ascertain the effectiveness of different models. Confusion matrices for three models are depicted in Table 4.

Table 4. Confusion matrices of models

Confusion matrices			
Models		Fake	Real
Transformer (BERT)	Fake	939	54
	Real	397	1151
LSTM with regularization	Fake	897	96
	Real	188	1360
CNN	Fake	893	154
	Real	38	1510
SVM	Fake	600	397
	Real	740	800
NB	Fake	605	388
	Real	746	802

Obtained accuracy from these five models is displayed in Table 5 and 6.

Table 5. Comparison of overall performance among models

Evaluation matrices	Fake news detection models				
	Transformer (BERT)	LSTM with regularization	CNN	SVM	NB
AUC	95%	88%	92%	61%	55%
Precision	0.95	0.82	0.95	0.44	0.44
Recall	0.94	0.90	0.84	0.60	0.61
F1 score	0.94	0.85	0.89	0.50	0.51

Table 6. Comparison of performance among models for fake news detection

Evaluation matrices	Fake news detection models				
	Transformer (BERT)	LSTM with regularization	CNN	SVM	NB
Precision	95%	82%	95%	44%	44%
Recall	93%	90%	84%	60%	61%
F1 score	94%	85%	89%	50%	51%

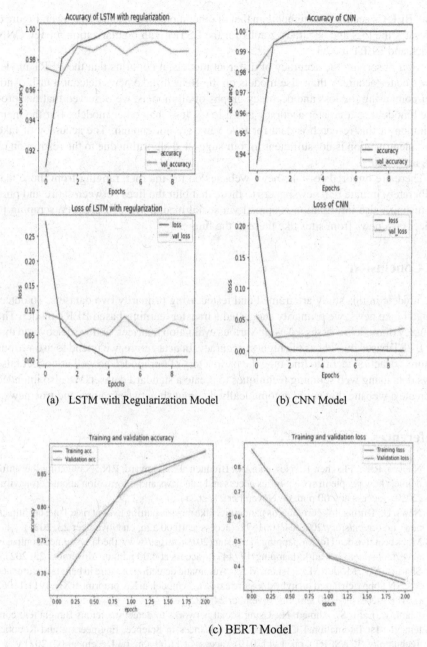

(a) LSTM with Regularization Model   (b) CNN Model

(c) BERT Model

Fig. 6. Accuracy and loos graph of models

After comparing the results of several performance matrices in Tables 4, 5 and 6 we show that BERT model outperforms all others. We also calculate the loss and accuracy of three models that achieve good results in the detection of fake news in Bengali. Among them, BERT's accuracy is higher than that of other models, and its loss is lower. Figure 6 illustrates the loss and accuracy graphs for the LSTM with regularization model, CNN model, and BERT model.

After observing the accuracy of different models, it confirms that the BERT model shows better accuracy than else models on the Bengali fake news detection task. And, after comparing the loss and accuracy graphs of all models, we observed that our proposed model has a greater accuracy and a lower loss than other models. But the main limitation of this research is data for fake news are not enough. The accuracy of fake news identification is not sufficient for our suggested algorithm due to the restriction of fake news data.

There are hundreds of fake news websites on the internet, ranging from those that deliberately imitate real newspapers to those that blur the lines between satire and pure confusion. False information is spread via social media. We will use web scraping to collect fake news from sites like these in the future.

5   Conclusion

The models in this study are trained and tested using primarily two datasets. To detect Bengali fake news, we primarily suggested a transfer learning-based BERT model. The accuracy of models is assessed using various evaluation matrices, and we discovered that our BERT-based model has the highest accuracy. In near future, we intend to use various feature extraction tactic to fine-tune the parameters of our model, as well as collect false news data using web scraping techniques to create a standard dataset. We also intended to create a website that could automatically distinguish between phony and true news.

References

1. Nielsen, R.K., Fletcher, R., Newman, N., Brennen, J.S., Howard, P.N.: Navigating the 'info-demic': how people in six countries access and rate news and information about coronavirus (2020). (access at 9.00 p.m. on November 21, 2021)
2. News, U.: During this coronavirus pandemic, fake news is putting lives at risk: Unesco. https://news.un.org/en/story/2020/04/1061592. (access at 10.00 a.m. on November 23, 2021)
3. Mobs beat five dead for kidnapping, daily star (2019). https://www.thedailystar.net/frontpage/news/mobs-beat-2-dead-kidnapping-1774471. (access at 4.00 p.m. on November 23, 2021)
4. Sharma, A.S., Mridul, M.A., Islam, M.S.: "Automatic detection of satire in bangla documents: A CNN approach based on hybrid feature extraction model. arXiv preprint arXiv:1911.11062 (2019). (access at 9.00 a.m. on November 24, 2021)
5. Islam, T., Latif, S., Ahmed, N.: Using social networks to detect malicious Bangla text content. In: 1st International Conference on Advances in Science, Engineering and Robotics Technology (ICASERT), pp. 1–4 (2019). (access at 11.00 a.m. on December 02, 2021)
6. Shu, K., Bernard, H.R., Liu, H.: Studying fake news via network analysis: detection and mitigation. In: Agarwal, N., Dokoohaki, N., Tokdemir, S. (eds.) Emerging Research Challenges and Opportunities in Computational Social Network Analysis and Mining. LNSN, pp. 43–65. Springer, Cham (2019). https://doi.org/10.1007/978-3-319-94105-9_3
7. Hung, D.V., D'Souza, M. (eds.): ICDCIT 2020. LNCS, vol. 11969. Springer, Cham (2020). https://doi.org/10.1007/978-3-030-36987-3

8. Shu, K., Mahudeswaran, D., Liu, H.: Fakenewstracker: a tool for fake news collection, detection, and visualization. Comput. Math. Organ. Theory **25**(1), 6071 (2018). (access at 7.00 p.m. on December 06, 2021)
9. Torky, M., Nabil, E., Said, W.: Proof of credibility: a blockchain approach for detecting and blocking fake news in social networks. Int. J. Adv. Comput. Sci. Appl. **10**(12) (2019). https://doi.org/10.14569/IJACSA.2019.0101243. (access at 8.00 a.m. on December 10, 2021)
10. Shu, K., Wang, S., Liu, H.: Exploiting tri-relationship for fake news detection. arXiv:abs/1712.07709 (2017). (access at 11.00 a.m. on December 10, 2021)
11. Vedova, M.L.D., Tacchini, E., Moret, S., Ballarin, G., Pierro, M.D., de Alfaro, L.: Automatic online fake news detection combining content and social signals. In: 2018 22nd Conference of Open Innovations Association (FRUCT), pp. 272–279 (2018). (access at 8.00am on January 02, 2022)
12. Kaliyar, R.K., Goswami, A., Narang, P.: FakeBERT: fake news detection in social media with a BERT-based deep learning approach. Multimed Tools Appl. **80**, 11765–11788 (2021). (access at 4.00 pm on January 02, 2022)
13. Adhikari, A., Ram, A., Tang, R., Lin, J.: Docbert: Bert for document classification (2019). arXiv preprint arXiv:1904.08398. (access at 7.00 am on January 03, 2022)
14. Antoun, W., Baly, F., Hajj, H.: AraBERT: transformer-based model for Arabic language understanding (2020). arXiv preprint arXiv:2003.00104. (access at 9.00 am on January 03, 2022)
15. Jwa, H., Oh, D., Park, K., Kang, J.M., Lim, H.: exBAKE: automatic fake news detection model based on bidirectional encoder representations from transformers (BERT). Appl. Sci. **9**, 4062 (2019). https://doi.org/10.3390/app9194062.[accessat6.00pmonJanuary03,2022]
16. Hossain, M.Z., Rahman, M.A., Islam, M.S., Kar, S.: Banfakenews: a dataset for detecting fake news in Bangla (2020). (access at 7.00 am on January 05, 2022)
17. Md Rashidul, M.G.H., Mahmuda, R., Joy, P., Sakib, H.: Detection of Bangla Fake News using MNB and SVM Classifier (2020). (access at 7.00pm on January 05, 2022)
18. sagorsarker/bangla-bert-base · Hugging Face. (access at 8.00am on January 06, 2022)
19. Wolf, T., et al.: Hugging face's transformers: State-of-the-art natural language processing (2019). arXiv:abs/1910.03771. (access at 11.00am on January 06, 2022)
20. Kim, Y.: Convolutional neural networks for sentence classification. In: Conference on Empirical Methods in Natural Language Processing (EMNLP), pp. 1746–1751 (2014). (access at 9.00 am on January 07, 2022)
21. Shrestha, P., Sierra, S., Gonzalez, F., Montes, M., Rosso, P., Solorio, T.: Convolutional neural networks for authorship attribution of short texts. In: Proceedings of the 15th Conference of the European Chapter of the Association for Computational Linguistics, vol. 2, pp. 669–674 (2017). (access at 7.00 am on January 09, 2022)
22. Srivastava, N., Hinton, G., Krizhevsky, A., Sutskever, I., Salakhutdinov, R.: Dropout: A simple way to prevent neural networks from overfitting, J. Mach. Learn. Res. 15 1, 1929–1958 (2014). (access at 4.00pm on January 09, 2022)
23. Hochreiter, S., Schmidhuber, J.: Long short-term memory. Neural Comput. 9 8, 1735–1780 (1997). (access at 11.00 am on January 11, 2022)
24. Zhou, P., et al.: Attention-based bidirectional long short-term memory networks for relation classification. In: Proceedings of the 54th Annual Meeting of the Association for Computational Linguistics, vol. 2, pp. 207–212 (2016). (access at 9.00 am on January 12, 2022)
25. Devlin, J., Chang, M., Lee, K., Toutanova, K.: BERT: pre-training of deep bidirectional transformers for language understanding. CoRR, 2018.abs/1810.04805. (access at 10.00am on January 15, 2022)

26. Chakraborty, P., Ahmed, S., Yousuf, M.A., Azad, A., Alyami, S.A., Moni, M.A.: A human-robot interaction system calculating visual focus of human's attention level. IEEE Access **9** (2021)
27. Chakraborty, P., Yousuf, M.A., Zahidur Rahman, M., Faruqui, N.: How can a robot calculate the level of visual focus of human's attention. In: Uddin, M.S., Bansal, J.C. (eds.) IJCCI 2019. AIS, pp. 329–342. Springer, Singapore (2020). https://doi.org/10.1007/978-981-15-3607-6_27
28. Chakraborty, P., Muzammel, C.S., Khatun, M., Islam, S.F., Rahman, S.: Automatic student attendance system using face recognition. Int. J. Eng. Adv. Technol. **9**, 93–99 (2020)
29. Sayeed, S., Sultana, F., Chakraborty, P., Yousuf, M.A.: Assessment of eyeball movement and head movement detection based on reading. In: Bhattacharyya, S., Mršić, L., Brkljačić, M., Varghese Kureethara, J., Koeppen, M. (eds.) ISSIP 2020. AISC, vol. 1333, pp. 95–103. Springer, Singapore (2021). https://doi.org/10.1007/978-981-33-6966-5_10
30. Chakraborty, P., Yousuf, M.A., Rahman, S.: Predicting level of visual focus of human's attention using machine learning approaches. In: Shamim Kaiser, M., Bandyopadhyay, A., Mahmud, M., Ray, K. (eds.) Proceedings of International Conference on Trends in Computational and Cognitive Engineering: Proceedings of TCCE 2020, pp. 683–694. Springer Singapore, Singapore (2021). https://doi.org/10.1007/978-981-33-4673-4_56
31. Muzammel, C.S., Chakraborty, P., Akram, M.N., Ahammad, K., Mohibullah, M.: Zero-shot learning to detect object instances from unknown image sources. Int. J. Innov. Technol. Explor. Eng. **9**(4), 988–991 (2020)
32. Sultana, M., Ahmed, T., Chakraborty, P., Khatun, M., Hasan, M.R., Uddin, M.S.: Object detection using template and hog feature matching. Int. J. Adv. Comput. Sci. Appl. **11**(7) (2020). https://doi.org/10.14569/IJACSA.2020.0110730
33. Faruque, M.A., Rahman, S., Chakraborty, P., Choudhury, T., Um, J.S., Singh, T.P.: Ascertaining polarity of public opinions on Bangladesh cricket using machine learning techniques. Spat. Inf. Res. **30**, 1–8 (2021)
34. Sarker, A., Chakraborty, P., Sha, S.S., Khatun, M., Hasan, M.R., Banerjee, K.: Improvised technique for analyzing data and detecting terrorist attack using machine learning approach based on twitter data. J. Comput. Commun. **8**(7), 50–62 (2020)
35. Khalil, A., Shawon, J.A.B., Chakraborty, P., Md Islam, J., Islam, S.: Recognizing Bengali sign language gestures for digits in real time using convolutional neural network. Int. J. Comput. Sci. Inf. Secur. **19**(1) (2021)
36. Sultana, M., Chakraborty, P., Choudhury, T.: Bengali abstractive news summarization using Seq2Seq learning with attention. In: João, M.R., Tavares, S., Dutta, P., Dutta, S., Samanta (eds.) Cyber Intelligence and Information Retrieval: Proceedings of CIIR 2021, pp. 279–289. Springer Singapore, Singapore (2022). https://doi.org/10.1007/978-981-16-4284-5_24
37. Ahmed, M., Chakraborty, P., Choudhury, T.: Bangla document categorization using deep RNN model with attention mechanism. In: Tavares, J.M.R.S., Dutta, P., Dutta, S., Samanta, D. (eds.) Cyber Intelligence and Information Retrieval. LNNS, vol. 291, pp. 137–147. Springer, Singapore (2022). https://doi.org/10.1007/978-981-16-4284-5_13

Crowd Counting Using Federated Learning and Domain Adaptation

Radha Senthilkumar🆔, S. Ritika$^{(\boxtimes)}$🆔, Mridini Manikandan🆔, and B. Shyam🆔

Department of Information Technology, Madras Institute of Technology Campus,
Anna University, Chennai, India
`ritika.singaravelou@gmail.com`

Abstract. Crowd counting is a technique used to estimate the number of people in an image at a particular instance. Accurate and quick estimation of crowd counts is a challenging yet meaningful task which has a wide range of applications in diverse fields. A CNN-based crowd counting approach which utilizes the first 13 layers of pre-trained VGG-16 model and dilated convolutional layers to generate quality density maps is proposed. The dilated layers allow for larger receptive fields without increasing the amount of computation. In addition, a federated learning-based approach involving the federated averaging algorithm is adopted to decentralize the training process, reduce the time taken and preserve privacy. The problem of domain-adaptation in crowd counting is also addressed by training a model using the abundant labelled data available in the source domain and transferring the parameters learnt to a target domain with relatively fewer labelled data using neuron linear transformation, thereby minimizing the domain gap and improving performance.

Keywords: Crowd counting · CNN · Federated learning · Domain adaptation

1 Introduction

Crowds occur in a variety of situations, for instance, concerts, political campaigns, religious gatherings, rallies, marathons, and stadiums. Hence, it is important to devise an efficient method to estimate the number of people in an image. Crowd counting has proved to be extremely useful in real-world applications like urban planning, disease control, traffic management, public security, crowd analysis, and surveillance. It also helps in getting more accurate and comprehensive information critical for making swift decisions to prevent and mitigate stampedes and riots. Thus, crowd counting has emerged as an important research area with the potential to offer promising solutions.

The conventional methods for crowd counting include detection-based, region-based regression, and density estimation-based approaches. However, these traditional techniques face many challenges like high cluttering, variations in illumination and crowd densities, susceptibility to background interference, differences in resolutions and scales, blurring and occlusions. With advancements in the fields of deep learning and computer vision, CNN-based approaches [9] have also been developed. Federated learning-based methods can also be used to parallelly train models across clients and aggregate their results using federated averaging [11] to obtain a global model with better performance in lesser time. Such distributed learning-based crowd counting methods are useful as surveillance cameras are often installed in different geographical locations and gathering all training data at one place in real-time is expensive.

Existing crowd counting techniques often presume that crowd images are captured by the same camera from similar viewpoints, under the same lighting conditions and backgrounds, and have identical crowd densities. But this assumption is not very realistic. Moreover, the existing real-time datasets are limited in number and scale and are likely to cause degradation in performance. This gives rise to the need for generating a domain adaptation-based crowd counting method [8, 15] that exploits a source domain with a large amount of training data and uses transfer learning to minimize the domain gap and provide a model that is suitable for target domains with few-shot data.

2 Related Work

The methods used for crowd counting can be categorized as detection-based, regression-based, density estimation-based, and CNN-based methods.

Crowd counting methods based on detection make use of a sliding window detector to identify individuals in a specific image and return their count. For instance, the detection-based crowd counting method discussed in [1] focuses on detecting pedestrians in annotated, monocular images using various state-of-the-art detection algorithms. However, these approaches fail to perform well on highly congested crowd images with severe occlusion.

In regression-based methods, the crowd images are first cropped into patches. Following this, the low-level features are extracted from them and crowd count is calculated. For example, a multiple-output regression model for joint localized crowd counting is proposed in [2]. The inter-dependent low-level features from local spatial regions are learnt and local crowd count outputs are provided. However, saliency is usually ignored in these approaches. This results in incorrect predictions.

Density maps are first generated for the available crowd images in density estimation-based methods. Then, an algorithm is used to find the mapping between the local features extracted and the corresponding density maps. In [3], the random forest algorithm performs density estimation for the crowd counting task. All the patches from the input image are extracted and branching is carried out recursively until the leaf node is reached in order to obtain predicted labels. Using these labels, patch-level density maps are computed. The density map of the entire image is generated by taking the average of all overlapping predicted maps.

CNN-based methods allow for the entire crowd image to be processed end-to-end, unlike the previous approaches which worked at the patch level. In [4], predictions of deep and shallow convolutional networks are merged to perform crowd counting. The deep network is used to capture features on a higher level and its architecture is similar to that of VGG-16. The shallow network is used to recognize the low-level head blob features. This combination allows for obtaining accurate crowd counts under extreme variations. The proposed method in [5] uses Switching Convolutional Neural Network (Switch-CNN).

This method helps in reducing the crowd count error and improves density localization by utilizing the density variation from the input image. This method maps patches in a grid from a crowd image to independent CNN regressors. A switch classifier aids in sending the patch to the appropriate regressor. A method proposed to detect the crowd count from a single arbitrary image taken from any different perspective consisting of a varied crowd density is discussed in [6]. It utilizes a Multi-Column Convolutional Neural Network (MCNN) which has 3 convolutional neural networks columns with filters of varied sizes. This enhances the network's ability to account for variations in perspectives. The density maps are obtained accurately with the help of kernels that can adapt to the geometry of the crowd scene and bring about generalizability. A fully convolutional model is discussed in [7] to predict the number of people in an image. The absence of fully connected layers ensures that the spatial information is retained. This approach produces a density map which is of the same size as the input crowd image. An unbiased ground truth generation method is also introduced to overcome perspective distortions.

Often, adequate data is available in a particular domain while relatively scarce data is available in another domain. In numerous crowd counting applications, the concept of domain adaptation comes into play to ensure that a model performs well and predicts the crowd count accurately in a new target domain by leveraging the large amount of source domain data it was trained with. In order to enable domain adaptive crowd counting, a deep learning-based approach is introduced in [8]. The backbone architecture of Multi-Column Convolutional Neural Network is adopted with the intent to transform the models learned in one domain to a target domain, which varies from the former in various aspects like backgrounds, environment, lighting, viewpoints, etc. The concept of maximum mean discrepancy is incorporated as domain adaptation loss. Additionally, supervised, semi-supervised, and unsupervised domain adaptation methods have been performed considering various standard datasets as the source and target domains.

With the growing increase in the importance of privacy, the use of decentralized learning has increased. The issues of resource allocation, communication costs, and data security of a traditional machine learning model are resolved via a federated learning approach. In [11], federated learning has been used for image classification where the model trains a large image dataset distributed among 5 users on their own devices without sending the data to the server.

3 Proposed Work

3.1 Data Preprocessing-Ground Truth Density Map Generation

The objective of data preprocessing in the proposed work is to generate two-dimensional ground truth density maps using the space-wise distribution of people for all crowd images provided in the dataset in the form of matrices consisting of head annotations. For every head annotation in the matrix, the mean distance of its k nearest neighbors is computed. The head annotations in the image are blurred by convolving using a Gaussian filter normalized to 1. Thus, the ground truth density map is generated. The crowd count is computed by calculating the integral over the density map. Figure 1 shows a crowd image from the Shanghai Tech part B (STB) dataset. Figure 2 shows the ground truth density map generated for the same image.

Fig. 1. A crowd image from STB dataset   **Fig. 2.** Corresponding ground truth density map

3.2   CNN-Based Crowd Counting

The system architecture shown in Fig. 3 represents the steps involved in CNN-based crowd counting. The Shanghai Tech B dataset consists of crowd images and their head annotation matrices. These matrices are preprocessed in order to obtain ground truth density maps. These are used as labels while training the CNN model. The model is then evaluated using the mean absolute error metric.

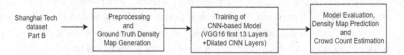

Fig. 3. Architecture diagram for CNN-based crowd counting

VGG-16 is a popular deep convolutional neural network model widely used in various deep learning image classification problems [16]. There are a total of 13 convolutional layers and 3 fully connected layers. The input to the model is a 224 × 224 RGB image. This is then passed through a stack of convolution layers. The first two layers are convolutional layers that use 64 filters and a pooling layer. This is followed by two convolutional layers having 128 filters and a max pooling layer. Three convolutional layers are also added with 256 filters and followed by a max pooling layer. This is added with two more stacks, each containing 3 convolutional layers having 512 filters and a max pooling layer. Finally, there are 2 fully connected layers and a softmax layer with an output of 1000 classes. All convolutional layers have a 3 × 3 filter with a stride of 1 and max pooling layers have a 2 × 2 filter of stride 2.VGG-16 uses small filters with added depth instead of large filters and still provides effective receptive field. It has found numerous applications in the area of computer vision. Figure 4 shows a detailed architecture diagram for the VGG-16 model [18].

In order to handle complicated problems and achieve better results, the CNN model is often deepened by stacking additional layers. However, this increases the number of parameters and can prove to be computationally expensive. The existence of pooling

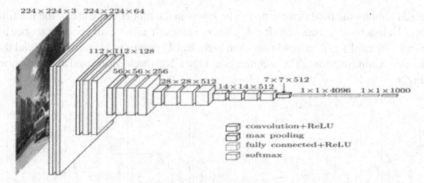

Fig. 4. VGG-16 architecture

layers also leads to the loss of resolution and hence reduction of the model's accuracy and performance. Dilated convolution layers act as an effective alternative [17]. They expand the kernel by inserting holes between its consecutive elements (pixel skipping). This enlarges the receptive field and offers more detailed information without increasing the number of parameters or the amount of computation. An additional parameter called dilation rate is used to indicate how much the kernel is widened. In dilated convolution, a small-size kernel with k × k filter is enlarged to k + (k − 1) (r − 1) x k + (k − 1) (r − 1) with dilation rate r. The use of dilated layers also proves to be computationally efficient as it offers wider field of view with every convolution operation and does not increase the number of parameters [9]. Figure 5 depicts the dilated kernels and their receptive fields for different dilation rates.

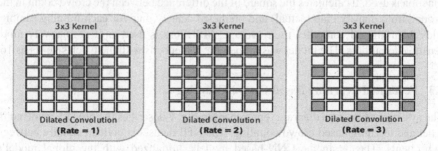

Fig. 5. Dilated kernels for different dilation rates

The proposed CNN model architecture uses a convolutional neural network consisting of the first 13 pre-trained layers of the VGG-16 backbone, followed by 6 layers of the dilated convolutional neural network and 1x1 convolutional layer. The first thirteen layers of the VGG-16 backbone are used for 2D feature extraction and the other deeper layers are avoided as they would lead to downgrading of the output by reducing its size in turn making it difficult for the generation of good quality density maps. The next six layers of the dilated convolutional neural network with dilated kernels process the extracted features efficiently with a dilation rate of 2. These layers are initialized using Gaussian initialization with 0.01 standard deviation. The final 1 × 1 convolutional layer is used to obtain the final density map. The layers in the model make use of the Rectified Linear Unit activation function (ReLU). Since it doesn't activate all neurons at once and prevents forwarding of values lesser than zero, ReLU proves to be more beneficial than other activation functions. The architecture of the CNN model discussed above is shown in Fig. 6.

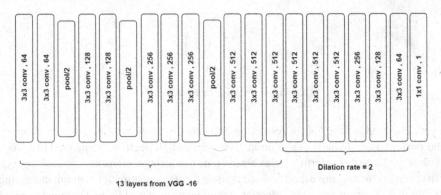

Fig. 6. CNN model architecture

Optimizers are algorithms used to change the attributes of a neural network like its learning rate or weights to minimize the error and maximize the efficiency of the model. For training the CNN model architecture shown in Fig. 6, the Adam optimizer is used and the learning rate is fixed to $1e-5$. In addition, the Mean Squared Error (MSE) loss function is used. It calculates the square of the difference between the crowd count in the ground truth density map (actual) and predicted density map for each training sample, adds them all and computes their average. MSE loss is used as it is relatively more sensitive to outliers. The model was trained for 100 epochs with the batch size set as 16.

3.3 Federated Learning Based Crowd Counting

The system architecture diagram represented in Fig. 7 describes the process involved in federated learning based crowd counting. The STB dataset is divided equally between two clients. They train the CNN-based models, initialized with the global model's weights, locally with their partition of data and share the training results to a global server. This server performs federated averaging of these models' weights and sends them back to the global model. This process is repeated in several rounds.

In traditional machine learning, the data and training are all done in a centralized location. However, federated learning allows for collaborative machine learning and eliminates the need for centralized training data. Federated averaging (FedAvg) is an algorithm used for distributed training with several clients. A random subset of members, called federated clients are selected and the training data is horizontally partitioned among them. Each client receives the global model synchronously from the server and computes an updated model using its local data. The model updates from all clients are forwarded to the central server, which then aggregates them to construct an improved

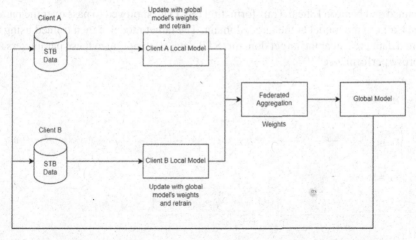

Fig. 7. System architecture for federated learning based crowd counting

global model, with better performance. The algorithm used for model aggregation is known as federated averaging. It involves component-wise parameter averaging which is scaled based on the proportion of data points (amount of data) contributed by each participating client. This procedure is repeated iteratively for the required number of communication rounds and the ultimate global model is obtained. Federated learning can be made more practical with the help of federated averaging which enables training of high-quality models using relatively fewer rounds of communication.

In the proposed work, horizontal federated learning is carried out. Two federated members (participating clients), namely client A and client B, are chosen and the Shanghai Tech Part B dataset is horizontally partitioned among them. The dataset contains 400 images for training and these are divided equally among both the clients. The CNN-based model discussed in the previous section is used here as well. To start with, clients will receive the current global model's weights from the server. At the client level, the local CNN model is trained using the client's data. Then, the model parameters obtained after training are aggregated. This model aggregation process involves the following steps. First, the resultant weights from local models trained by the clients, A and B, are scaled by multiplying them with a scaling factor. The scaling factor is calculated based on the amount of data contributed by each client. Here, the training data is shared equally among both clients. Hence, the scaling factor is 0.5. Then, the scaled weights of clients A and B are summed. This process is called federated averaging. These averaged weights are then updated to the global model. This marks the end of one communication round or global training epoch. This process is repeated for 100 communication rounds in order to obtain the final trained global model.

3.4 Domain Adaptive Crowd Counting

The system architecture diagram shown in Fig. 8 represents the process involved in domain adaptive crowd counting. The CNN model at the source domain (MALL dataset) is trained and Neuron Linear Transformation (NLT) is employed to pass over the parameters learnt to the model at the target domain. The target model is then trained using the limited data present at the target domain (STB dataset) to optimize these parameters and improve performance.

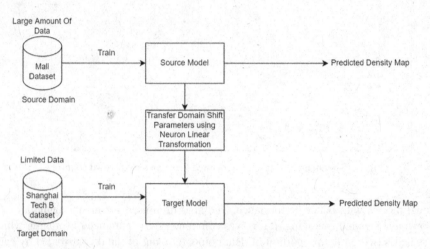

Fig. 8. System architecture for domain adaptation based crowd counting

Crowd images are often captured under varied lighting conditions, from different camera angles and contain diverse background elements. The crowd density in an image (whether the crowd is sparse or dense or highly congested) also varies to a great extent. The cameras used to click images also possess distinct features. For instance, two unique geographic locations which have cameras installed in real-time for capturing crowd images. The crowd images obtained from these two locations are bound to be different from each other. Therefore, a domain shift exists between them and a model that predicts accurate density maps using images from one location may not perform as well in the other. This dissimilarity amongst domains calls for a solution that can transfer the knowledge learnt from one domain to another in order to achieve better performance. This is the idea behind domain adaptation. Consider a source domain and a target domain, wherein the source domain contains a larger amount of labelled training data and the target domain contains insufficient data. The objective of domain adaptation is to map the domain shift between the two domains and transform the model learnt in the source domain to perform well in the target domain as well.

In the proposed work, supervised domain adaptation has been carried out. The source domain has several labelled images and greater diversity in terms of crowd density, lighting conditions, etc. while the target domain has few-shot labelled data, i.e., limited labelled images. The source and target domains were selected based on the number of labelled training images available in popular crowd counting datasets. The source domain used in this work is the MALL dataset which consists of over 1000 labelled training images and greater variation in activity patterns and scene objects. The target domain used is Shanghai Tech Part B dataset which has 400 labelled training images.

MALL dataset also has higher perspective distortion and more severe occlusions when compares to STB.

The method of Neuron Linear Transformation is utilized to delineate the gap between the two domains at the parameter level. In the proposed work, MALL dataset and STB dataset were chosen as the source and target domains. The same CNN-based model is considered at both the domains and called as source and target models. The source model is first trained and performs really well in the source domain. Then the target model is trained and NLT is embedded into this training process. The domain shift is thus modeled by transferring neurons from the source model to the target model which has lesser data. The target neuron is generated through a linear transformation. Ultimately, a target model is obtained which performs equally well in the target domain.

4   Results and Discussions

4.1   Datasets

Shanghai Tech Part B. The Shanghai Tech Part B (STB) dataset is a large-scale crowd counting dataset. It contains 716 annotated images with relatively sparse crowd scenes taken from metropolitan streets in urban areas of Shanghai, China.

MALL. The Mall dataset is a publicly accessible dataset predominantly used for crowd counting. Its images are collected from a surveillance camera located in a shopping mall. It includes 2,000 annotated video frames with an average resolution of 320×240. A total of 62,325 pedestrians are annotated in this dataset.

4.2   Evaluation Metrics

The evaluation metric used is Mean Absolute Error (MAE). MAE is the average of the absolute values of prediction error on each crowd image in the test data. Prediction error refers to the difference between the actual and the predicted values for a particular instance.

$$MAE = \frac{1}{N} \sum_{i=1}^{N} |C_i - C_i^{GT}| \tag{1}$$

where N is the number of images used for testing, C_i and C_i^{GT} are the predicted crowd count and the ground truth (actual) crowd count corresponding to the ith image.

In order to assess and examine the quality of the predicted density maps, PSNR (Peak Signal-to-Noise Ratio) and SSIM (Structural Similarity in Image) metrics are used. The SSIM value typically ranges from 0 to 1. Higher values of PSNR and SSIM indicate that the density maps are of good quality.

$$PSNR = 10.\log_{10}\left(\frac{MAX_i^2}{MSE}\right) \tag{2}$$

where MAX$_I$ is the maximum possible pixel value of the image and MSE (Mean Square Error) is defined as

$$MSE = \frac{1}{mn} \sum_{i=0}^{m-1} \sum_{j=0}^{n-1} [I(i,j) - K(i,j)]^2 \qquad (3)$$

where I is a $m \times n$ monochrome noiseless image and K is its noisy approximation.

$$SSIM(x,y) = [l(x,y)]^\alpha . [c(x,y)]^\beta . [s(x,y)]^\gamma \qquad (4)$$

where l is luminance, c is contrast, s is the structure and α, β, γ are the positive constants. Luminance, contrast and structure can further be defined as

$$l(x,y) = \frac{2\mu_x\mu_y + C_1}{\mu_x^2 + \mu_{y+}^2 C_1} \qquad (5)$$

$$c(x,y) = \frac{2\sigma_x\sigma_y + C_2}{\sigma_x^2 + \sigma_{y+}^2 C_2} \qquad (6)$$

$$s(x,y) = \frac{\sigma_{xy} + C_3}{\sigma_x\sigma_y + C_3} \qquad (7)$$

where μ_x and μ_y are local means, σ_x and σ_y are standard deviations and σ_{xy} is cross-covariance for images x and y.

4.3 Outcomes and Comparative Analysis

All three crowd counting approaches are evaluated using the Mean Absolute Error metric and the results are compared. The crowd image chosen for testing and its corresponding ground truth density map are shown in Fig. 9 and Fig. 10 respectively. The original crowd count for this image is 87.

Fig. 9. Original image   Fig. 10. Ground truth density map

The three crowd counting methods discussed earlier, namely CNN-based crowd counting, federating learning-based crowd counting and domain-adaptive crowd counting are used to predict the density map and hence, estimate the number of people in an image. In order to effectively compare these methods based on their ability to generate accurate density maps, the same image from the STB dataset is used for testing. The predicted density maps for each approach are shown in Figs. 11, 12 and 13.

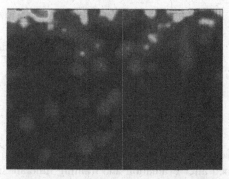

Fig. 11. The density map predicted using CNN with dilation layers whose crowd count is 99.32

Fig. 12. The density map predicted using federated learning whose crowd count is 97.11

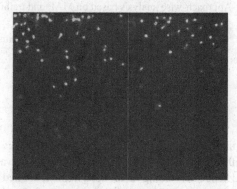

Fig. 13. The density map predicted using domain adaptation whose crowd count is 79.48

Table 1 represents the crowd count estimated based on the density maps predicted for each of the three crowd counting approaches used.

Table 1. Approach-wise analysis based on predicted crowd count

Approach	Original crowd count	Predicted crowd count
CNN with dilation layers	87	99.32
Federated learning	87	97.11
Domain adaptation	87	79.48

The approaches used for crowd counting in this paper and their corresponding Mean Absolute Error obtained after evaluation and training time are listed in Table 2. The lower the MAE, the more accurate the approach is. The crowd counting approach that uses a CNN based architecture with dilation layers gave the least value of Mean Absolute Error (10.99) within a moderate training time (4.5 h). Federated learning-based crowd counting is found to have the shortest training time (2.5 h) along with a slightly higher MAE (11.13). The short training time for this approach can be attributed to the fact that training data is divided among various clients and the training process occurs at different locations and devices simultaneously. The domain adaptive crowd counting approach has a reasonable MAE (21.49) but the time taken for training (7 h) is considerably long. Here, the source model is first trained in a source domain with a huge amount of training data. Transferring the knowledge gained in this process to a target model with lesser data is a time-consuming and elaborate process. This explains the training time of 7 h. In addition, performance of a model often depends on the amount of data available for training. Since, the target domain has fewer data, the domain adaptation-based approach results in the highest MAE among the three approaches.

Table 2. Approach-wise analysis based on MAE and training time

Approach	MAE	Training time
CNN with dilation layers	10.99	4.5 h
Federated learning	11.13	2.5 h
Domain adaptation	21.49	7 h

In federated learning-based crowd counting, the training data is horizontally divided among federated members or clients. As the number of clients are varied, their individual data contributions and hence the scaling factor used in the federated averaging algorithm also varies. Table 3 describes how the counting error and training time change when the number of clients is varied. As the number of clients increases, the number of models' whose weights will be scaled and averaged will also increase. This excessive averaging can lead to increase in MAE. Moreover, greater duration of time will be required to train the local models and send their weights to the global server. This explains the increase in training time as the number of federated clients increases.

The quality of density maps generated is pertinent to the accuracy of the crowd counts obtained. The standard metrics used to evaluate density map quality are PSNR and SSIM.

Table 3. Comparison based on number of federated clients

No. of clients	MAE	Training time
2	11.13	2.5 h
3	27.85	3.6 h
4	14.24	4.1 h

The PSNR and SSIM values calculated for each of the crowd counting approaches used are compared in Table 4.

Table 4. Approach-wise comparison of PSNR and SSIM

Approach	PSNR	SSIM
CNN with dilation layers	31.11	0.91
Federated learning	31.23	0.90
Domain adaptation	26.82	0.81

5 Conclusion and Future Work

5.1 Conclusion

In this work, a deep CNN-based architecture that allows for generation of quality density maps and hence, accurate crowd counts using images from congested crowd settings captured in the Shanghai Tech B dataset, is proposed. The use of dilated convolutional layers as a replacement for pooling layers allows for a greater receptive field and minimal loss of resolution. The proposed model was also extended to federated-learning and domain-adaptation-based crowd counting approaches. The federated-learning approach involved training the model with local data at the client level, exchanging the resultant parameters and aggregating them, and then updating the global model. The process was repeated iteratively to obtain improved results. The domain-adaptive crowd counting approach facilitated the transfer of knowledge gained from a large and diverse source domain to a relatively few-shot target domain. In this work, the task of crowd counting has been carried out using three different approaches. It has been observed that in terms of MAE alone, the "CNN with dilation layers" approach is the best (MAE = 10.99) and when training time alone is taken into consideration, the federated learning approach with 2 federated clients provides the best result (Training time = 2.5 h). At the same time, competent results were obtained when a crowd counting model trained at one domain is put to use in another domain with lesser data using the "Domain Adaptive" approach.

5.2 Future Work

The work to be carried out in the future involves improving the quality of crowd density maps produced, making them look more visually appealing and reducing the mean absolute error further to obtain more accurate crowd counts. Furthermore, the current work deals with static-image based crowd counting only. Domain adaptive crowd counting can also be implemented for other datasets as well as images collected from real-world source and target domains that vary based on camera angle, location, etc. The work can be expanded to video-based crowd counting in real-time to facilitate various practical applications. Addition of crowd monitoring, segmentation, tracking and localization capabilities can also be done in the future.

References

1. Dollar, P., Wojek, C., Schiele, B., Perona, P.: Pedestrian detection: an evaluation of the state of the art. IEEE Trans. Pattern Anal. Mach. Intell. **34**(4), 743–761 (2012)
2. Chen, K., Loy, C., Gong, S., Xiang, T.: Feature mining for localised crowd counting. In: Proceedings of the British Machine Vision Conference (2012)
3. Pham, V., Kozakaya, T., Yamaguchi, O., Okada, R.: COUNT forest: CO-voting uncertain number of targets using random forest for crowd density estimation. In: IEEE International Conference on Computer Vision (ICCV) (2015)
4. Boominathan, L., Kruthiventi, S., Babu, R.: CrowdNet: a deep convolutional network for dense crowd counting. In: Proceedings of the 24th ACM international conference on Multimedia (2016)
5. Sam, D., Surya, S., Babu, R.: Switching convolutional neural network for crowd counting. In: IEEE Conference on Computer Vision and Pattern Recognition (CVPR) (2017)
6. Zhang, Y., Zhou, D., Chen, S., Gao, S., Ma, Y.: Single-image crowd counting via multi-column convolutional neural network. In: IEEE Conference on Computer Vision and Pattern Recognition (CVPR) (2016)
7. Wang, J., Wang, L., Yang, F.: Counting crowd with fully convolutional networks. In: 2017 2nd International Conference on Multimedia and Image Processing (ICMIP) (2017)
8. Hossain, M., Reddy, M., Cannons, K., Xu, Z., Wang, Y.: Domain adaptation in crowd counting. In: 2020 17th Conference on Computer and Robot Vision (CRV) (2020)
9. Li, Y., Zhang, X., Chen, D.: CSRNet: dilated convolutional neural networks for understanding the highly congested scenes. In: 2018 IEEE/CVF Conference on Computer Vision and Pattern Recognition (2018)
10. Wang, Q., Han, T., Gao, J., Yuan, Y.: Neuron linear transformation: modeling the domain shift for crowd counting. IEEE Transactions on Neural Networks and Learning Systems, pp. 1–13 (2021)
11. Hrushi, P., Tapan, D. and Jeya, R.: Federated learning for image classification using federated averaging algorithm. Annals of RSCB, pp. 5610–5615 (2021)
12. Yang, Q., Liu, Y., Chen, T., Tong, Y.: Federated machine learning. ACM Trans. Intell. Syst. Technol. **10**(2), 1–19 (2019)
13. Chen, X., Bin, Y., Sang, N., Gao, C.: Scale pyramid network for crowd counting. In: 2019 IEEE Winter Conference on Applications of Computer Vision (WACV) (2019)
14. Kong, D., Gray, D., Tao, H.: A viewpoint invariant approach for crowd counting. In: 18th International Conference on Pattern Recognition (ICPR 2006) (2006)

15. Wang, Q., Gao, J., Lin, W., Yuan, Y.: Learning from synthetic data for crowd counting in the wild. In: 2019 IEEE/CVF Conference on Computer Vision and Pattern Recognition (CVPR) (2019)
16. Simonyan, K., Zisserman, A.: Very Deep Convolutional Networks for Large-Scale Image Recognition. arXiv preprint arXiv:1409.1556 (2014)
17. Chen, L., Papandreou, G., Kokkinos, I., Murphy, K., Yuille, A.: DeepLab: semantic image segmentation with deep convolutional nets, atrous convolution, and fully connected CRFs. IEEE Trans. Pattern Anal. Mach. Intell. **40**(4), 834–848 (2018)
18. VGG16 - Convolutional Network for Classification and Detection. https://neurohive.io/en/popular-networks/vgg16. Accessed 12 July 2022w

News Headline Generation Using Abstractive Text Summarization

Jeetendra Kumar[1]([✉]) [iD], Shashi Shekhar[2] [iD], and Rashmi Gupta[1] [iD]

[1] Atal Bihari Vajpayee University, Bilaspur, Chhattisgarh, India
jeetendragupta@bilaspuruniversity.ac.in
[2] GLA University, Mathura, India

Abstract. People's willingness to read is declining at an alarming rate as their attention spans decrease. Consequently, crafting a brief description of the most significant news story, as well as the most intuitive title that relates to the synopsis, is key concept. When individuals write summaries of articles, they do not only take words and concatenate them, they also make up new grammatical phrases or sentences that are grammatically comparable to the original piece and communicate original gist of text. Despite the fact that humans have a great ability to abstract information, automated summarization is a challenging task. To produce news headlines from a corpus of news articles, an abstractive text summarization-based approach has been developed. Abstractive text summarization is a suitable fit for this goal since it produces human-like summaries. The seq2seq approach is often employed in abstractive text summarization. The proposed method Seq2Seq model with LSTM for generation of news headlines. ROUGE and BLEU scores have been used to evaluate performance of the model. The proposed approach also performs better in terms of ROUGE and BLEU scores, when compared with other state of art news headline generation methods.

Keywords: Summarization · News headline · Seq2Seq · Abstractive · Text summary

1 Introduction

The most common way of developing a compact, precise, and familiar rundown of extended text content is known as text summarization. To help users select important information and consume it more quickly, automatic text summarising is need of the hour to manage large amount of text available on digital platforms. For some decades, it has been seen that a vast amount of digital data is being generated day to day. According to a report of statistica [1], till 2025 180 zb data will be generated globally. Due to this vast amount of data, and it has become very difficult to find the relevant information in his own interest. When users search the information on the internet, it provides thousands of data, some are relevant and some are irrelevant. To find the informative data, users need to read the entire document and waste the time reading that document. In many cases, users have no time to read the entire text. So text summarization provides an easy-to-use method for generating summarized text. Text summarization system increase the effectiveness of the document, reduces the reading time, increases the productivity level and ensures that all important facts are covered in summary.

In some decades, many researchers are working exhaustively in the area of text summarization and many business products are in the market for text summarization. According to a market report [2], global text analytic market will reach to 14.84 billion till 2026. From this trend, it can be assumed that there is a lot of scope for research work in this area.

Some problems are associated with text summarization. Some of the primary issues addressed in the process of text summarising include text identification, interpretation, and summary production, as well as analysis of the created summary. Identifying key terms in the document and using them to find relevant information to include in the summary is one of the most important jobs in extraction-based summarization. Some challenges like performance matrix for summary quality assessment, domain specific summaries, generating concise summaries are associated with text summarization. The majority of effective text summarising systems uses extractive summarization. Abstraction-based summarization is intrinsically more complex, and it is a research topic in progress.

Text Summarization Can Be Done Using Two Approaches

- **Extractive text summarization -** Extractive summarization methods are focussed to identify important lines in large text. These important lines are combined to generate a brief summary
- **Abstractive text summarization (ATS) -** Abstractive text summarization generates the new sentence itself from the piece of text. Those sentences may not be present in the text. The abstractive method generated text is shorter and conveys the information to the original text. Abstractive text summarization reduces grammatical inconsistency of the text document. ATS methods uses models of natural language processing to generate brief summary.

In this paper, a model has been developed to generate news headlines using the abstractive text summarization method on news article corpus that can generate short-length news headlines. The dataset has been extracted from 'inshorts' news websites. This dataset contains a large number of news data like headlines, text, author, date, and read_more attributes. Before building the model, many pre-processing techniques have been applied to the dataset to make the data ready for processing. For model building, Seq2Seq model with LSTM has been used. To measure the efficiency of the model, ROUGE score and BLEU score have been used.

2 Literature Review

Text summarization is not a very new area of research. A lot of work has been already done in the area of text summarization. Earlier extractive text summarization techniques have been used for text summarization but these techniques did not produce exactly human-like summaries because some sentences are selected from text to produce a summary. Nowadays abstractive text summarization techniques are being used because they produce human-like summaries. We have discussed some abstractive text summarization techniques here. Recent works on abstractive text summarization use the seq2seq model; they are quite suitable to solve the text summarization problem. Rush et al. [3] proposed ATS with attention mechanism. They used the neural language model with a generation algorithm with the DUC 2003 and DUC 2004 datasets. They used the data extracted from the New York Times. This model produces accurate abstractive summarization. Nallapati et al. [4] used attention encoder-decoder Recurrent Neural Network as well as hierarchical attention model for abstractive text summarization. In their work, they used annotated Gigaword corpus as described in Rush et al. [3]. At the decoding time, they used beam search to size 5to generate the summary. The dataset they used is CNN/DailyMail dataset and DUC corpus (2003). The limited size of the summary to a maximum of 30 words but these models produce summaries that contain repetitive phrases at times. To overcome these problems they used the temporal attention model of Sankaran et al. [5]. They also establish benchmark numbers of future work. Narayan et al. [6] used a Convolutional Neural network and multi-hop attention model for a single-document summarization task. They construct the real-world large-scale dataset by harvesting online articles from the British Broadcasting Corporation (BBC). This model creates a short and one-sentence new summary and generates the text-summaries whose length is 90 tokens. Talukder et al. [7], generate the abstractive text summary using seq2seq model with bi-directional LSTM with attention model. They used the Bengali dataset extracted from social media sites such as Facebook etc. This model provides the maximum accurate predicted summary. For creating text summaries, Liu et al. [8] employed LTABS, a novel sequence to sequence model (Abstractive Summarization on LSTM and transformer). The transformer is better suited for summary generating activities with this model. CNN and DailyMail, as well as XSum, were utilised as datasets. The words in the original text can be copied using the LTABS model. This approach also produces a fantastic text summary from the lengthy material. Toi Nguyen et al. [9] applied an encoder convolutional neural network. In their work, they introduce an architecture called pointer-generation E-Con (PGEC) whose conditioning is the combination between pointer generator and a novel convolutional network with weight normalization. They used two datasets Gigaword and DUC (2004) dataset, and perform ROUGE 1 score. ROUGE 1 score on the Gigaword dataset is 32.28 and on the DUC (2004) is 27.13. This model produces an abstractive summary without the repetition of words. K.R. Mishraet al. [10] applied sequence to sequence encoder-decoder model using RNN and bidirectional Gated Recurrent Unit (GRU) method. GRU method used for their capability of learning long-term dependencies. In this work, they used the Nepali news articles and headlines are scraped from different Nepali news web portals. This model is carried out with proper word vector representation and the approach can be well used for Nepali text generation. Zepeng Hao et al. [11] used feature-enhanced seq2seq model for text summarization. The capture network is used in this model to improve the encoder and decoder in traditional seq2seq, and the second feature is used to increase the model's capacity to retain long-term and global characteristics. The CNN Daily Mail dataset was utilized. This approach compresses longer content into a concise, high-quality summary.

Mohamed Youssfi et al. [12] used RNN with encoder-decoder. They also used their owed trained French word embedding. A novel headline creation approach based on a generative pre-trained model was suggested by Ping et al. [13]. This model just includes a decoder that includes the pointer mechanism and n-gram language information. The dataset was created using data from the Chinese micro blogging site sinaweibo, and it was given the label big scale Chinese short text summary (LCSTS). The source text was shortened to 80 tokens and title was shortened to 10 tokens. The proposed work have used seq2seq with just LSTM model and encoder- decoder with LSTM for news summary using abstractive text summarization. For evaluating the performance, ROUGE-1, ROUGE-2, ROUGE-L and BLEU scores have been used. ROUGE measures recall and BLEU measures precision.

3   Methodology

In this study, a model for generating short-length news headlines has been built utilizing the abstractive text summarization approach on a news article corpus. The dataset has been extracted from the 'inshorts' news website. The headlines, text, author, date, and read more characteristics are all present in this dataset. Many pre-processing approaches were used on the dataset before developing the model to prepare it for processing. The headline generation model have been created using Seq2Seq model with LSTM and has been implemented in Tensor Flow TPU version. TPU has far more processors than the CPU. ROUGE and BLEU scores were used to assess the model's efficacy. The workflow of the methodology is shown in Fig. 1.

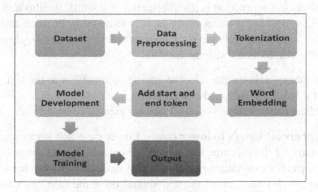

Fig. 1. Workflow of process

3.1   Dataset

To build a model news headline generation, huge data is required to produce a better result. The dataset has been extracted from 'inshort' news website using API. This dataset contains several columns such as text, headlines, author, date and read_more, but only text and headlines column have been used in the proposed work. This dataset contains 29358 Data instances. Following Table 1 shows some characteristics of the data.

Table1. Characteristics of data

	Minimum length of text in characters *	Maximum length of text in characters *	Average length of text in characters*
Text	280	417	360
Headline	34	99	70

* Including spaces.

3.2 Data Pre-processing

Datapre-processing is one of the important parts of text analytics because it cleans and prepares the text for analysis. There are many methods of data pre-processing but the use of all these methods are depended on the objective of the model and type of data. A regular expressions have been used to remove the unwanted data from news text along with spacy. Pipe () method to take advantage in the form of speed. Following Fig. 2 shows pre-processing steps used in the proposed method.

Fig. 2. Pre-processing steps

Add contractions – Contraction is the shortening of a word, such as *don't* for *do not* and *aren't* for *are not*. For a better analysis, it is required to broaden this contraction in the text data. You may simply get a contractions dictionary on Google or make your own and map the contractions with the module.

The following example shows the effect of adding contractions to the text.
Original Text - "y'all can't expand contractions".
Text after adding contractions - 'you all can not expand contractions'.

Converting uppercase letters to lower case - Lower case and upper case letters are viewed differently by the machine and a machine can easily read the words if the text is in the same case, for example, the computer distinguishes between the terms life and Life. To prevent such issues, all of the text should be in the case, with the lower case being the most preferable case. So in the proposed method, all upper case letters are converted to lower case letters. The following example shows the effect of converting uppercase letters to lowercase letters.

Original Text: Tamil Nadu launches free vaccination drives
Converted Text: tamilnadu launches free vaccination drives

Remove words containing digits - When words and digits are mixed in a document, it might be difficult for robots to grasp. As a result, words and numerals that are concatenated, such as sports12 or password@111, must be removed. Because this sort of term is difficult to understand, it is best to eliminate it or replace it with an empty string.

Removal of stopwords - Stopwords do not add anything to the conversation. The NLTK library is a widely used library for removing stopwords. It eliminates about 180 stopwords.

Original Text: "World-class drainage system will be developed in India".
Text after removal of stopwords: "world-class drainage system developed India".

Removal of Special Symbols – Some special symbols like @, #, &, * etc. also have been removed from the text and summary.

3.3 Tokenization

Tokenization is the process of dividing text into smaller chunks, such as individual words or phrases. A "token" is a term used to describe each of these smaller parts. In this work, fit_on_text tokenizer has been used that is part of the Keras tokenizer class, which is used to update internal vocabulary for the text list. The rare word analysis is also performed on text and summary parts of data.

Output of rare word analysis on text
{'percent': 61.27, 'total_coverage': 5.67, 'count': 26005, 'total_count': 42446}
Output of rare word analysis on summary
{'percent': 72.56, 'total_coverage': 10.76, 'count': 13066, 'total_count': 18006}

3.4 Word Embedding

A numeric vector input that represents a word in a lower-dimensional space is referred to as Word Embedding or Word Vector. It permits the display of words with comparable meanings. They can also be used to make educated guesses about what is being spoken. A 50-valued word vector can express 50 distinct characteristics. Individual words in a word embedding are represented as real-valued vectors in a specified vector space. The technique is usually combined with deep learning since each word is mapped to a single vector, and the vector values are obtained in a way that mimics a neural network. Each unique word is represented as a real-valued vector in a predetermined vector space when utilising words embeddings. In this work, one hot encoding word embedding has been used. One hot encoding vector is a format in which a vector's just one bit is 1. If the corpus contains 500 words, the vector length will be 500. We take a window size and cycle over the whole corpus after assigning vectors to each word. After tokenizing, the vocabulary size of the text was 42,447, and the vocabulary size of the summary was 18007. A collection of all words and their associated embedded terms is called an embedded matrix. Size of embedding matrix for text was found (42548, 300) and size of embedding matrix for summary was found (18061, 300).

118   J. Kumar et al.

3.5 Add Tokens to Identify the Beginning and Ending of Text

To mention the start and end of the text some special tokens such as <sostok> and <eostok> have been used. It is important to use <sostok> and <eostok> as start and end tokens respectively because TensorFlow's Tokenizer will filter the tokens and convert them to lowercase. If _START_ & _END_ symbols will be used to mention the start and end of text then tf's tokenizer will convert them to start and end respectively. For example, in the sentence 'start everything is going to end in 2020 end', the tokenizer will help when will stop decoding when the first 'end' was found. So both _START_ & _END_ and <sostok> and <eostok> have been used in the proposed work for better identification of the start and end of the text.

3.6 Model

There is a lot of deep learning model used for different purpose like machine translation, text classification, sentiment classification, etc. In the proposed work, seq2seq model with LSTM has been used. This paradigm may be applied to any sequence-based issue, particularly those in which the inputs and outputs are of varying sizes and categories.

Seq2Seq Model - Sequence to Sequence models are a type of Recurrent Neural Network architecture that is commonly used to address complicated language issues such as Machine Translation, Question Answering, Chatbot creation, Text Summarization, and so on. Seq2seq takes a sequence of words (sentences or sentences) as an input and creates a sequence of words as an output. The recurrent neural network is used to do this (RNN). Although the basic RNN is rarely utilized, the more complex versions, such as LSTM or GRU, are. This is due to the vanishing gradient issue that RNN has. In Google's planned version, LSTM is employed. By accepting two inputs at each moment in time, it constructs the word's context. The name recurring comes from two sources: one from the user and the other from the prior output (output goes as input). Seq2Seq model is a learning model that converts an input sequence into an output sequence as shown Fig. 3.

Let us consider that x and y stand for the input and output sequences. The item at i^{th} position of input sequence is xi, and the item at j^{th} position of the output sequence is yj. In general, x_i and y_j vectors are the one-hot vectors representation of text. The one-hot vector symbolizes the word, and the size of the vector becomes the vocabulary size.

Consider the seq2seq paradigm in the context of natural language processing (NLP). Let the vocabulary of the inputs and outputs be V(s) and V(t), respectively, and all the elements xi and yj fulfil $x_i \in R^{|V(s)|}$ and $y_i \in R^{|V(t)|}$. The following equations depict the input sequence X and the output sequence Y.

$$x = (x_1, ..., x_I) = (x_i)_{i=1}^{I}$$

$$y = (y_1, ..., y_J) = (y_j)_{j=1}^{J}$$

The lengths of the input and output sequences are represented by I and J, respectively. y_0 is the one-hot vector of SOS, which is the virtual word representing the beginning of the sentence, and y_{J+1} is the one-hot vector of EOS, which is the virtual word representing the conclusion of the sentence, in usual NLP notation.

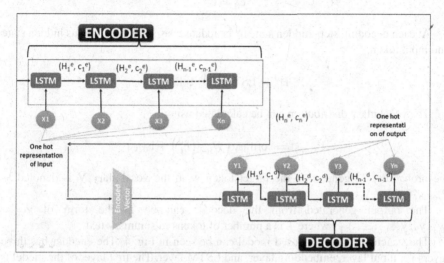

Fig. 3. Seq2Seq model with encoder and decoder

Seq2seq model has mainly two components:

Encoder - The seq2seq model is constructed using encoder-decoder architecture. The one hot representation of input sequence to passed to the encoder part. The encoder generally consists of many LSTM or GRU units. At every timestamp, one word of input sequence passed to the encoder. Each unit of LSTM, generated cell state, hidden state and output state. In encoder, cell state and hidden states are passed to the next unit and output state is discarded. The final cell state and hidden state are passed to decoder. The states are used to initialize to the decoder.

The above diagram shows the structure of the encoder part of the model. The encoder consists of LSTM cells. The encoder part of the seq2seq model reads source text. The source text can be represented in the form of $x = (x_1, x_2, x_3, \ldots\ldots x_n)$. . When source text is processed by LSTM units the output of the cell is discarded and hidden state (h^e) and cell (c^e) are passed to the next LSTM unit. At the end of the encoding source text is converted to a hidden state. The hidden states can be represented as $h^e = \left(h_1^e, h_2^e, h_3^e, h_4^e, \ldots\ldots h_n^e\right)$ and cell states can be represented as $c^e = \left(c_1^e, c_2^e, c_3^e, c_4^e, \ldots\ldots c_n^e\right)$ where n is the number of tokens in the source text. Here it can be said that the number of tokens in the source text and the number of hidden states is the same. These hidden states and cell states i.e. $\left(h_n^e, c_n^e\right)$ are passed to the decoder to produce output.

Decoder - Decoder is an LSTM whose initial states are initialized to the final states of the Encoder LSTM i.e. $\left(h_n^e, c_n^e\right)$.

The initial state of decoder can be initialized as follows.

$$h_0^d = \tanh\left(W_{e2d}\left(h_j^e\right) + b_{e2d}\right)$$

$$c_0^d = c_j^e$$

At each decoding step, hidden state h_t^d is updated based on the previous hidden state and input token.

$$H_t^d = LSTM\left(h_{t-1}^d, E_y^t\right)$$

The vocabulary distribution can be calculated using

$$P_{vocab}t = softmax\left(W_{d2v}\left(h_t^d\right) + b_{d2v}\right)$$

the probability of generating the target token w in the vocabulary V is denoted as $P_{vocab}, t\,(w)$.

The output generated from the decoder can be in the form of $y = (y_1, y_2, y_3, \ldots \ldots y_T)$ where T is a number of tokens in summary text.

The structure of the proposed model can be seen in Fig. 4. The encoder has three layers i.e. input layer, embedding layer, and LSTM layer. The first layer of the model is the input layer. The output shape of the input layer is [(None, 42)] where the maximum length of the text is 42. The next layer of the model is the embedding layer. In embedding layer taken three inputs i.e. input dimension, output. Input dimension is the size of the vocabulary of text which is 42447 for our model. Output dimension is size vector space in which word will be embedded which is 300 for our model. All weights are initialized with an embedding matrix of text. The output shape of the embedding layer is (None, 42, 300). In the encoder, one LSTM layer has been used. This LSTM layer has 240 nodes. The output of the embedding layer works as input for LSTM layer. Output shape of LSTM layer is [(None, 42, and 240), (None, 240), (None, 240)]. Then encoder returns outputs, hidden states, and cell states. These outputs are discarded and hidden states and cell states are passed to the decoder. In the decoder, three-layer i.e. embedding layer, LSTM layer, and output layer have been used. The first layer of the decoder is the embedding layer. In the embedding layer, the input dimension is 18007, which is the vocabulary size of the summary. In the embedding layer output dimension is 300. The weight of embedding layers is initialized with an embedding matrix of summary. The output shape of the embedding layer is [(None, None, 300)]. In the decoder, one LSTM layers and one output layer have been used. Each LSTM layer has 240 nodes. The output layer is a dense layer with a softmax activation function.

4   Results and Analysis

To evaluate the performance of the proposed model for news headline generation, ROUGE and BLEU scores have been used. These scores are used to measure the efficiency of text summarization and machine translation. For this, ROUGE-1, ROUGE-2,

```
Model: "model"
_____
Layer (type)                  Output Shape        Param #    Connected to
=================================================================================
input_1 (InputLayer)          [(None, 42)]        0          []

embedding (Embedding)         (None, 42, 300)     12839100   ['input_1[0][0]']

input_2 (InputLayer)          [(None, None)]      0          []

lstm (LSTM)                   [(None, 42, 240),   519360     ['embedding[0][0]']
                               (None, 240),
                               (None, 240)]

embedding_1 (Embedding)       (None, None, 300)   5440500    ['input_2[0][0]']

lstm_1 (LSTM)                 [(None, 42, 240),   461760     ['lstm[0][0]']
                               (None, 240),
                               (None, 240)]

lstm_2 (LSTM)                 [(None, None, 240), 519360     ['embedding_1[0][0]',
                               (None, 240),                   'lstm_1[0][1]',
                               (None, 240)]                   'lstm_1[0][2]']

time_distributed (TimeDistribu (None, None, 18135) 4370535   ['lstm_2[0][0]']
ted)
=================================================================================
Total params: 24,150,615
Trainable params: 11,311,515
Non-trainable params: 12,839,100
```

Fig. 4. Structure of the model

and ROUGE-L; Individual 1-g BLEU score, Individual 2-g BLEU score, Individual 3-g BLEU score, Individual 4-g BLEU score; Cumulative 1-g BLEU score, Cumulative 1-g BLEU score, Cumulative 1-g BLEU score, Cumulative 1-g BLEU score, Cumulative 1-g BLEU score have been used. Obtained values of score are shown Table 2, Table 3 and Table 4.

ROUGE score (R score) - ROUGE stands for "Recall-Oriented Understudy for Gisting Evaluation". "R-Score includes measures to automatically determine the quality of a summary by comparing it to other (ideal) summaries created by humans" [14]. This metric counts the number of overlapping units, between the computer-generated summary and the summary generated by humanbeings.

ROUGE-N (R-N) - It measures unigram, bigram, trigram, and other higher-order overlapping units.

ROUGE-1 (R-1) measures unigram overlap and ROUGE-2 measures bigram overlap.

ROUGE-L (R-L) This score computes the longest matching sequence of words using the longest common sequence (LCS). The benefit of the LCS is that it does not need consecutive matches, but rather in-sequence matches that indicate sentence-level word order. It does not require a predefined n-gram length since it automatically comprises the longest in-sequence common n-grams. The following equations show the R-N scores formula.

$$R - Nscore = \frac{\sum_{\{S \in Refrence\_summary\}} \sum_{gram_n} count_{match}(gram_n)}{\sum_{\{S \in Refrence\_summary\}} \sum_{gram_n} count(gram_n)}$$

Table 2. ROUGE score

ROUGE score	
R-1	48.83
R-2	20.48
R-L	40.32

BLEU score (B-score) - BLEU score stand for "Bilingual Evaluation Understudy Score". It is short matrices for evaluation generating summary with reference summary. Perfect match results 1.0 BLEU score and perfect mismatch score results 0.0 B - Score. B - Score is expensive to calculate, easy to understand, independent from language and correlates highly with human evaluation. In the NLTK BLEU score computations, you may set the weighting of different n-grams in the B-score calculation. This allows you to compute various B-scores, such as individual and cumulative n-gram ratings. For Individual-1 g (I-1 g) match, weight will be (1,0,0,0), for Individual-2 g (I-2 g) match, weight will be (0,1,0,0), for Individual-3 g (I-3 g) match, weight will be (0,0,1,0), and for Individual-4 g (I-4 g) match, weight will be (0,0,1,0). The cumulative n-gram B-Score is computed using the sentence bleu() and corpus bleu() scores. For the 1-g, 2-g, 3-g, and 4-g scores, the weights are 1/4 (25%) or 0. Following table shows individual N-GRAM individual B-Score and N-Gram cumulative B-Score.

Table 3. Individual BLEU scores

N-gram individual bleu score result	
I-1g	0.32'
I-2 g	1.00
I-3 g	1.00
I-4 g	1.00

Table 4. Cumulative BLEU scores

N-cumulative bleu score tresult	
C-1 g	0.32
C-2 g	0.52
C-3 g	0.69
C-4 g	0.75

The proposed method for news headline generation is also compared with other state of art methods to access the level of performance. From the following Table 5 and Fig. 5, it can seen that proposed method performed better than the other discussed methods. The method SHEG [15] is based on a hybrid method of text summarization i.e. combined approach of extractive and abstractive summarization. The suggested approach extracts the most important phrases and then combines the power of a pointer–generator network and CAC (Controlled actor critic) model to create an abstractive summary, which is then utilized to create a headline that conveys significant information while still being intriguing enough to pique a reader's interest. The method HG-NEWS [13] was not based on an encoder-decoder model but it has used only an encoder. This method employs multihead attention to get the semantic representation of input tokens as well as the attention distribution on those tokens. In this news headline production model, there is a robust feature input module that incorporates mood and part of speech characteristics. The method CNHG [16] was based on zero-shot learning. They suggested a reinforcement learning system that consists of two modules that seek to handle the cross-lingual headline production problem by utilizing current same-language headline-generating training data and translation training data. In our proposed method, an abstractive text summarising technique was used on a news article corpus to build a model for generating short-length news headlines in this work. Using data from the 'inshorts' news website, the dataset is created. This dataset comprises, among other things, headlines, text, author, date, and read more characteristics. Before creating the model, the dataset was subjected to a variety of pre-processing procedures to prepare it for processing. The model was created using the Seq2Seq model with LSTM.

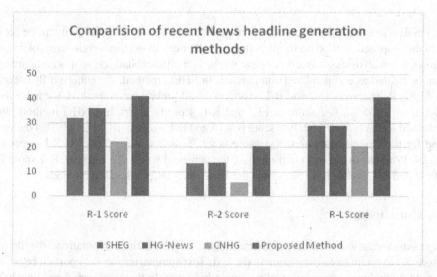

Fig. 5. Performance comparison of recent headline generation methods

The above methods based on the ROUGE score because most of the methods have calculated ROUGE score only as a performance measure. In the proposed method,

Table 5. Performance comparison of recent headline generation methods

Work	Dataset used	Summarization type	Methodology	R-score
SHEG [15]	CNN Daily mail Gigaworld Newsroom	Hybrid	Extractive+Reinforced abstractive mechanism	R-1 - 31.82 R-2 - 13.2 R-L -28.80
HG-News [13]	LCSTS	Abstractive	Seq2Seq model with attention	R-1 - 35.80 R-2 - 13.7 R-L - 28.80
CNHG [16]	Self developed Chinese-English dataset DUC2004 Gigaword	Abstractive	Zero shot model based neural headline generation	On DUC 2004 dataset R-1 - 20.62 R-2 - 4.16 R-L - 18.02 On Gigaword dataset R-1 - 22.35 R-2 - 5.64 R-L -20.29
Our method	Our dataset extracted from inshort news website	Abstractive	Seq2Seq model with LSTM	R-1- 48.80 R-2 – 20.48 R-L - 40.32

ROUGE score and BLEU score, both are calculated. From the Table 5, it can be seen that the proposed method performs better than other discussed methods in terms of rouge scores. Even all discussed methods have worked on different datasets so this comparison can be treated as a generalized comparison. In SHEG method, the achieved R-1 score is 31.82, R-2 score is 13.2 and R-L scores is 28.80. In HG-News method, the achieved R-1 score is 35.80, R-2 score is 13.7 and R-L score is 28.80. In CNHG method, the achieved R-1 score is 20.62, R-2 score is 4.16 and R-L score is 18.02 DUC 2004 dataset and for the Gigaword dataset, R-1 score is 22.35, R-2 score is 5.64 and R-L score is 20.29. Whereas in the proposed method, the achieved R-1 score is 48.80, R-2 score is 20.48 and R-L scores is 40.32, which are better than other discussed methods.

5 Conclusion

Text summarization is the task of shortening the length of data computationally with an objective to retain key information in the text. Text summarization is important because it reduces the unnecessary time of reading a long text. In this work, an abstractive text summarization-based method has been used to generate news headlines from the news article corpus. The abstractive text summarization is suitable for this task because it generates human-like summaries. In abstractive text summarization, seq2seq model is commonly used. In this work, seq2seq model with LSTM has been used. For the purpose of evaluation of performance, ROUGE and BLEU scores have been used. Proposed method was also found better than recent methods in terms of ROUGE score and BLEU score. In the future, work on cross-language summarization can be done.

References

1. Total data volume worldwide 2010–2025 | Statista. https://www.statista.com/statistics/871 513/worldwide-data-created/. Accessed 06 Jan 2022
2. Text Analytics Market Size (2021–26) | Industry Share, Growth - Mordor Intelligence. https://www.mordorintelligence.com/industry-reports/text-analytics-market. Accessed 07 Jan 2022
3. Rush, A.M., Chopra, S., Weston, J.: A neural attention model for abstractive sentence summarization. In: Proceedings of the EMNLP 2015, vol. 1509, no. 685, pp. 1–11, September 2015
4. Nallapati, R., Zhou, B., dos Santos, C., Gulçehre, Ç., Xiang, B.: Abstractive text summarization using sequence-to-sequence RNNs and beyond. In: CoNLL 2016 - 20th SIGNLL Conference on Computational Natural Language Learning Proceedings, pp. 280–290, February 2016
5. Sankaran, B., Mi, H., Al-Onaizan, Y., Ittycheriah, A.: Temporal attention model for neural machine translation, August 2016
6. Narayan, S., Cohen, S.B., Lapata, M.: Don't give me the details, just the summary! Topic-aware convolutional neural networks for extreme summarization. In: Proceedings of the 2018 Conference on Empirical Methods in Natural Language Processing, EMNLP 2018, pp. 1797–1807, August 2018
7. Mohammad Masum, A.K., et al.: Abstractive method of text summarization with sequence to sequence RNNs. In: 2019 10th International Conference on Computing, Communication and Networking Technologies, ICCCNT 2019, July 2019
8. Liu, X., Xv, L.: Abstract summarization based on the combination of transformer and LSTM. In: Proceedings of the 2019 International Conference on Intelligent Computing, Automation and Systems, ICICAS 2019, pp. 923–927, December 2019
9. Nguyen, T., Le, T., Tran, N.T.: Abstractive sentence summarization with encoder-convolutional neural networks. In: Proceedings of the 2020 12th International Conference on Knowledge and Systems Engineering, KSE 2020, pp. 13–18, November 2020
10. Mishra, K.R., Rathi, J., Banjara, J.: Encoder Decoder based Nepali news headline generation. Int. J. Comput. Appl. **175**(20), 975–8887 (2020)
11. Hao, Z., Ji, J., Xie, T., Xue, B.: Abstractive summarization model with a feature-enhanced seq2seq structure. In: 2020 5th Asia-Pacific Conference on Intelligent Robot Systems, ACIRS 2020, pp. 163–167, July 2020
12. Erraki, M., Youssfi, M., Daaif, A., Bouattane, O.: NLP summarization: abstractive neural headline generation over a news articles corpus. In: 4th International. Conference on Intelligent. Computing in Data. Sciences, ICDS 2020, October 2020
13. Li, P., Yu, J., Chen, J., Guo, B.: HG-news: news headline generation based on a generative pre-training model. IEEE Access **9**, 110039–110046 (2021)
14. Lin, C.-Y.: ROUGE: a package for automatic evaluation of summaries, pp. 74–81 (2004)
15. Singh, R.K., Khetarpaul, S., Gorantla, R., Allada, S.G.: SHEG: summarization and headline generation of news articles using deep learning. Neural Comput. Appl. **33**(8), 3251–3265 (2020)
16. Ayana, Chen, Y., Yang, C., Liu, Z., Sun, M.: Reinforced zero-shot cross-lingual neural headline generation. IEEE/ACM Trans. Audio Speech Lang. Process. **28**, 2572–2584 (2020)

Facial Based Age Estimation Among Dark Skinned Hominid Species

Berlinda Asiedu[1], Justice Kwame Appati[2]([⊠]) [iD], and Winfred Yaokumah[2] [iD]

[1] Department of Computer Science and Information System, Ashesi University, 1 University Avenue, Berekuso, Ghana
berlinda.asiedu@ashesi.edu.gh
[2] Department of Computer Science, University of Ghana, Legon, Accra, Ghana
{jkappati,wyaokumah}@ug.edu.gh

Abstract. By intuition humans can estimate the age of an individual effortlessly. However, this task can be very challenging for face age recognition system. These challenges primarily are attributed to the unavailability and the underrepresentation of appropriate dataset used in the training of age estimation models. A specific scenario is the underrepresentation of black race which raise the concern of algorithm accountability resulting in inefficient model formulation. In this study, a dataset named Faces was curated from secondary sources containing face images of the black race. A hybrid model consisting of a KNN classifier and an SVR was then proposed to estimate these ages. For a fair comparison, the trained hybrid model was experimented on three other datasets and compared to the LARR model which was the state-of-the-art model at the time of study. The results showed that the proposed model generated the least MAE on the Faces dataset which affirms our hypothesis that a model works better with the kind of data used curated.

Keywords: SVR · KNN · Hybrid algorithm · Feature extraction · Age estimation · Face images · Black race · Human faces · Hominid age · Classifiers

1 Introduction

The recognition of humans is mostly based on their biometric features such as the iris, fingerprint, face, and DNA. However, the looks of a person may change over time due to factors such as ageing, wrinkles, beard growth, the difference in weather conditions and facial expressions. These characteristics play a key role in building face and age recognition systems especially among the black race for security, forensics, surveillance monitoring, and commerce. Unfortunately, these age estimation systems are underutilized in areas where they mostly seem inaccurate and inefficient. Studies have shown that, the underrepresentation of face images of black people in age estimation system has posed the threat of algorithm accountability and its biasedness terms of race. In this study we identify and study the various algorithms for age estimation, while analyzing their accuracy in detecting and estimating the ages of blacks using face images.

C. Badica et al. (Eds.): ICICCT 2022, CCIS 1670, pp. 126–136, 2022.
https://doi.org/10.1007/978-3-031-20977-2_10

Furthermore, a dataset is curated along with a proposed hybrid model. In the study, a pipeline for secondary data collection, integration of images and pre-processing, facial landmarking and feature extraction, and age estimation using the proposed hybrid model was discussed.

2 Related Works

The estimation of human age can be done with different biometric features; however, the focus of this study is centered on face image data. In literature, several kinds of image can be estimated [1, 5, 14, 17]. Among them are chronological/actual age, perceived age, and appearance age. The objective of age estimation is to approximate as close as possible to the appearance age [2, 8, 13]. However, the challenge here is the pre-processing of the image against the presence or absence of facial hairs, glasses, and viewpoint differences [9, 10, 12]. In the study of [7] a hybrid model was proposed by combining the residual network with face embedding method using a triplet loss function. Using a labeled face in the Wild dataset, coupled with a 22 layered Inception Network for feature extraction, and accuracy of 99.5% was achieved. In [4], the authors proposed a hybrid method to estimate the correct age or age range of faces. In the proposed method, image quality enhancement, feature extraction, orientation and feature scaling were considered as pre-processing task. Further, the wrinkles in the face were extracted as features for age determination. Using a multi-SVM classifier, the age of the individual was estimated. The study of [11] also proposed a deep learning technique for age estimation which is independent of facial landmarks and wrinkle features. In the study IMDB-WIKI, FG-NET, MORPH, CACD, and LAP dataset were used. The proposed method is dependent on VGG-16 architecture as a pre-trained model for image classification. Experimentally, the method resulted in an average MAE or 3.09 for all the dataset used. The key performance of method is its ability to deeply learn from large data, computation of expected age regression and robust face alignment [15, 16]. Finally, the study of [6] classified faces as either aged, baby, or youth. However, it is well established that an age estimation system cannot guarantee a 100% accuracy as a result of different ageing patterns of different people due to some factors such as health, weather condition, diverse photography artefacts in image acquisition, and lifestyle. This observation makes this research domain open with the quest for researchers to develop a more efficient and accurate algorithms.

3 Materials and Research Models

This study's methodology follows the pipeline in Fig. 1, and each step is explained in detail in the following sections.

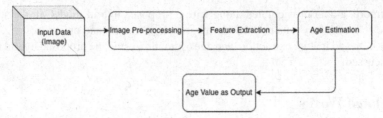

Fig. 1. Pipeline of methodology

3.1 Face Datasets

In this study, face images of black people serve as inputs for training and testing purposes. Most face datasets available at the study time contain very little or no black people's images. As the kind and amount of data used for training a model are essential for efficiency and accuracy, there is the need to create a dataset having the most significant proportion of it belonging to people of the black race. These images are gathered using the secondary data collection approach. Unfortunately, these secondary datasets found are hybrid (mixture of blacks and whites face data) in nature. However, since the focus of this study is on dark skinned face image, the study considered it appropriate to separate the black race from the hybrid data and put together to form a new dataset (FaceDB). FaceDB comprises 640 images from five different datasets: Age DB, Fair Face, MORPH-II, FG-NET, and the Chicago Face Dataset. Though in literature these databases are used in isolation in their hybrid form, this study also considers it necessary to introduce more heterogeneity to the data curated to test the robustness of the current study. The number of images per constituent dataset is displayed in Table 1, while sample images from the collated DB are shown in Fig. 2.

Table 1. Images in the dataset

Dataset	AgeDb	Morph-II	Fair face	Chicago face	FG-NET
Number of images	330	12	150	143	5

3.2 Image Processing

Images from the dataset are first preprocessed since not all the image data is centered appropriately. This process help align the detected faces for training and testing. The process also aids in efficient face landmarking, feature extraction and face detection. A comparable size of 400 * 400 is chosen for this study, and all images are resized to that effect. Further image pre-processing is done using Python's Open CV.

Greyscale Conversion and Rotation. The human face is known to contain 68 identifiable landmarks used for face detection applications such as age estimation. To obtain

Fig. 2. Sample face images

these landmarks, the face images are converted into greyscale and rotated to be centre aligned. Normalization of the image is done by rotating the face clockwise at an angle θ along the center of the eyes using Eq. 1. The image centre point is (γ_x, γ_y).

$$\theta = \tan^{-1}\left(\frac{RE_y - LE_y}{RE_x - LE_x}\right) \tag{1}$$

After the image is rotated, the right eye coordinate resolves to Eq. 2–3 and the left eye coordinate is given by Eq. 4–5.

$$RE_x^1 = \gamma_x + (RE_x - \gamma_x) \cdot \cos(\theta) - (RE_y - \gamma_y) \cdot \sin(\theta) \tag{2}$$

$$RE_y^1 = \gamma_y + (RE_x - \gamma_x) . \sin(\theta) - (RE_y - \gamma_y) . \cos(\theta) \tag{3}$$

$$LEx^1 = \gamma_x + (LE_x - \gamma_x) . \cos(\theta) - (LE_y - \gamma_y) . \sin(\theta) \tag{4}$$

$$LE_y^1 = \gamma_y + (LE_x - \gamma_x) . \sin(\theta) - (LE_y - \gamma_y) . \cos(\theta) \tag{5}$$

where (RE_x^1, RE_y^1) is the coordinate of the right eye, (LE_x^1, LE_y^1) is the coordinate of the left eye, and (γ_x, γ_y) is the center point. Finally, Eq. 2–5 is used to define the distance transform l of the center point between the eye center of the face ROI as expressed in Eq. 6.

$$l = \left(\left(RE_x^1 - LE_x^1\right)^2 + \left(RE_y^1 - LE_y^1\right)^2\right)^{\frac{1}{2}} = \left|RE_x^1 - LE_x^1\right| \tag{6}$$

Segmentation. In this study, segmentation is done to eliminate the need for individual pixel sorting and to facilitate image analysis.

Marker Labelling. This process is engaged to label multiple regions into their respective fields, thus background or foreground after which a watershed algorithm is employed. All "unknown" regions are labelled zero (0) while object boundaries are labelled −1.

3.3 Facial Land Marking and Feature Extraction

Pre-processed images undergo facial landmarking and feature extraction, which is required for machine learning algorithm. A python library (Dlib) is used to estimate the 68 landmarks on the face, and these features are extracted using the Gabor filters and Linear Discriminant Analysis (LDA). The Gabor filter is used for wrinkle, edge, and texture feature extraction. Linear Discriminant Analysis (LDA) on the other hand helps identify features that differentiate target classes from one another. The method is a linear combination of independent features to achieve the most suitable mean difference between the target classes. Mathematically, the within-class scatter matrix is given by Eq. 7.

$$S_w = \sum_{j=1}^{c} \sum_{i=1}^{N_j} (x_{ij} - \mu)(x_{ij} - \mu_j)^T \tag{7}$$

where c is the number of classes, x_{ij} is the ith sample of class j, N_j is the number of samples in class j and μ_j is the mean of class j. On the hand, the between-class scatter matrix is given by Eq. 8.

$$S_b = \sum_{j=1}^{c} (\mu_j - \mu)(\mu_j - \mu)^T \tag{8}$$

where μ is the mean of all classes. The objective of this algorithm is to maximize Eq. 8 while minimizing Eq. 7.

3.4 Age Estimation

The age estimation problem can be identified as a regression or classification problem. From a classification point of view, age range serves as the labels for each class, and as a regression problem, the ages can be considered a single whole number value, one for each image. Each of these approaches has certain demerits that can be catered for using a hybrid model. A hybrid model is a combination of a classification and regression model. The hybrid model provides robustness by using each algorithm to make up for the shortcomings of the other.

Classification Algorithms. Features extracted for each image during the feature extraction phase are fed into Machine Learning algorithms used as part of training models. Three different classifiers are tested and evaluated to get the most suitable classifier for this age estimation problem. These are the KNN Classifier, Decision Tree Classifier, and the Naïve Bayes.

KNN Classifier. The K-Nearest Neighbour algorithm (KNN) is a standard and efficient method for classifying objects related to the data closest to them in the training data in terms of their features or any independent variables. KNN is an instance base machine learning algorithm whose function is estimated locally and has all computations delayed until a class is obtained. In KNN, an object is given a class label depending on the class most prevalent among its k nearest neighbours. *"k"* is a positive integer, usually odd, representing the number of neighbours of the object being classified. For classification, a try and error method is used to determine the most suitable class for the object. Generally, having a more significant number of the fork helps reduce inaccuracies due to noise but makes the boundaries between classes similar. The accuracy of the KNN classifier can be affected by irrelevant features or if the features are inconsistent with their relevance.

Decision Tree Classifier. The Decision Tree Classifier is considered one of the optimal algorithms for classification. The classifier uses a tree-like structure with nodes named from the bottom as the root to the top leaf. The root node represents attributes, and the leaf nodes, represent class variables. The leaf nodes also represent the kind of class distribution being used. The decision tree classifier describes the relationship between the different attributes and their relative importance. It adopts the use of easily under-standable and implantable rules and does not require any complex data representation. Simple operators such as IF, IF-ELSE, AND, and OR are used in its implementation.

Naïve Bayes Classifier. Bayesian classifiers are statistical classifiers that estimate an object's class by identifying the probability of the object belonging to a particular class. The Classifier is one of the two fundamental Bayesian Classifiers developed with the Bayesian Networks. Naïve Bayes algorithms assume that an attribute's effect on a class is independent of other attributes' values which is termed as the conditional indepen-dence assumption. These classifiers are commonly used for classification because of their simplicity, outstanding performance, and computational efficiency for real-world problems.

Regression Algorithms. Estimating age as a regression problem is usually done in several ways. However, in this study, Logistic Regression, Age-Group-Specific Linear Regression (ALR), Multi-Layer Perceptron (MLP), Quadratic Regression (QR), and Support Vector Regression (SVR) is considered for discussion.

Support Vector Regression (SVR). The task of SVR is to find a function $f(y)$ such that its deviation (ϵ) from the target value (z_i) when given a training dataset is large and linear. In effect all error estimates less than ϵ are neglected. This observed char-acteristic makes the SVR model robust to outliers. Now given the dataset $D = \{(y_1, z_1), \cdots, (y_n, z_n)\}$, where $y_1 \in R^d$ and $z_1 \in R$, a linear function $f(y)$ can be approximated such that the optimal regression function is modeled as Eq. 9

$$min_{w,\varepsilon} \frac{1}{2}\|w\|^2 + C \sum_{i=1}^{n}\left(\xi_i^+ + \xi_i^-\right) \tag{9}$$

subject to $z_i - (w, y_i) - b \leq \varepsilon + \xi_i^+ (w, y_i) + b - z_i \leq \varepsilon + \xi_i^- \xi_i^+, \xi_i^- \leq 0$

where constant $C > 0$ determines the tradeoff between the flatness of f and data devi-ations, and ξ_i^+, ξ_i^-, are slack variables to cope with otherwise infeasible constraints on the optimization problem. However, in practice, the primal problem is solved more efficiently in its dual formulation, resulting in the final solution given, as Eq. 10 and 11.

$$w = \sum_{i=1}^{n}(\alpha_i - \alpha_i^*)y_i \qquad (10)$$

and

$$f(y) = \sum_{i=1}^{n}(\alpha_i - \alpha_i^*)(y_i, y) + b \qquad (11)$$

where α_i, α_i^* are Lagrange multipliers.

A non-linear (SVR) function can be obtained by using kernels, just as is done for a non-linear support vector machine (SVM) for classification. The kind of kernel used for a non-linear SVR depends on the nature of the problem. The different kernels that can be used are polynomials, sigmoid, or Gaussian radial basis functions. The Gaussian radial basis function kernel, for robust age regression, is more efficient than the linear regression because the linear regression is unable to model complex ageing processes. A Gaussian radial basis function is of the form as expressed in Eq. 12.

$$k(y, y^1) = e^{-\gamma \|y - y^1\|^2} \qquad (12)$$

where γ is a constant to adjust the width of the Gaussian function, the solution of the non-linear SVR, given the kernel mapping, is obtained in Eq. 13 and 14.

$$(w, y) = \sum_{i=1}^{n}(\alpha_i - \alpha_i^*)k(y_i, y) \qquad (13)$$

and

$$f(y) = \sum_{i=1}^{n}(\alpha_i - \alpha_i^*)k(y_i, y) + b \qquad (14)$$

The difference between the function for the non-linear regression and that of the linear regression is that w is not given explicitly. Also, in non-linear regression, the optimization problem seeks to find the flattest or linear graph.

Quadratic Regression (QR). A quadratic regression model can define the relationship between the extracted features, y, and the age labels, L, given the extracted landmarks for each face image Eq. 15.

$$L = f(y) \qquad (15)$$

The quadratic regression function for age regression, as seen in Eq. 16.

$$\hat{L} = \omega_o + w_1^T + w_2^T y^2 \qquad (16)$$

where $\hat{L}$ is the estimated age, ω_0 is the offset, and y *and* y^2 are the extracted feature vector and its square, and w_1 and w_2 are weight vectors. The model parameters are optimized by reducing the difference between the real ages of the images, L, and the ages estimated using $\|L - \hat{L}\|$. The loss function corresponds typically to a least square estimation (LSE) criteria.

4 Results and Discussion

4.1 Training

Every machine learning model learns features by being trained on a set of data before predicting objects' values by learning the relationships between variating features. The Faces dataset needs to be divided into two sets for training and testing the model. One set represents the training set, and the other represents the test set. The training set is the set of data used to train the algorithm for the model for age estimation. The other set is the testing set on which the model is tested to check for predicted ages' correctness. Comparing the results of testing and training helps avoid overfitting, where the model can accurately predict values for the training data but cannot do so for the testing data. 640 images were pre-processed, and 552 images were returned for training. These 552 images were divided into 80% for training and 20% for testing. This makes the training set a total of 442 images and the testing set, 110 images. After the division of the dataset is completed, the set of images for training is further split into subsets to prevent any overfitting resulting from the possibility of only one kind of data being in the training set. This is done using cross-validation. Cross-validation involves splitting the training set further into k subsets, k being 10 in this case, and training on k-1 subsets. The leftover subset is used for validation. Cross-validation is done using K-Folds Cross-Validation (K-Folds). A model that yields the best accuracy score is chosen for the hybrid model when this is done. Different regression and classification models are checked for how well they fit the age estimation problem of the training data. The evaluation metric used for classifiers is the accuracy score, and for regressors, the mean absolute error is used. Tables 2 and 3 show each model's cross-validation score, indicating how well they fit the problem. Figure 3 also present the boxplot of the four selected algorithms.

Table 2. Cross-validation scores of regression models

Method	LSVR	LR	SVR	MLPR
MAE	20.13	18.458	17.409	22.106

4.2 KNN-SVR Hybrid Algorithm

Age estimation as a classification and regression (hybrid) problem can be quite challenging. This challenge mainly arises from choosing the most suitable classifier and regressor to form the hybrid model. One may decide to select different algorithms and compare their accuracies on the same dataset. Locally adjusted robust regression (LARR) is one such hybrid model for age estimation. This model comprises a Support Vector Machine as a classifier and Support Vector Regressor. The LARR is tested on the YGA and FG-NET datasets, and results are evaluated using the mean absolute error metric. The results generated MAEs of 5.25 years for females and 5.30 years for males on the YGA database and 5.07 years on the FGNET ageing database. Training is proceeded

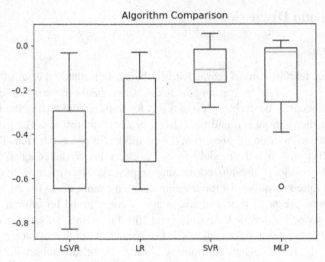

Fig. 3. Boxplot of regression model scores

Table 3. Cross-validation scores of classification models

Method	LDA	KNN	CART	NB	PER	SVC
Accuracy score	0. 62	0. 80	0.62	0.23	0.14	0.34

with using the classifier and regressor with the least MAE regression score, 17.409, and confusion matrix and highest accuracy score, 0.80. Support Vector Regression and KNN classifier are chosen as the models for the hybrid approach for age estimation using face images of the black race.

4.3 Discussions

In testing the model on 20% of the curated data, the performance of the model is determined using metrics such accuracy, the mean absolute error and the regression score. The results of the tests are shown in Tables 4 and 5.

Table 4. Performance evaluation scores of SVR

Model	MAE	R2
SVR	12.12	−0.06

From Tables 4 and 5, an accuracy value of 85% was recorded when the KNN classifier is employed while a mean absolute error of 12.12 was noted for the SVR. However, in

Table 5. Performance evaluation scores of KNN

Model	Accuracy
KNN	0.85

this study we proceeded to hybridize these two approaches (SVR and KNN) to create a new model (SVR+KNN). The SVR is used as robust global regressor while the KNN is used to locally adjust the age range after regression. In a similar study by [3], a locally adjusted robust regression (LARR) was proposed for image-based human age estimation. Applying the proposed method (SVR+KNN) and LAAR on AgeDB, Fair Face, and Faces the MAE is recorded in Table 6. In this section the Fair Face and AgeDB is used as it has a fair distribution of dark race images in them.

Table 6. MAE scores from experiment

Dataset	Age DB	Fair face	Faces
KNN+SVR	11	12.21	7.25
LARR	10	9.91	13
Error difference	*1*	*2.3*	*−5.75*

Comparing the two results in Table 6, one will observe that the LARR perform well over the proposed method on AgeDB and Fair Face, however, the proposed method outperforms LARR using the Faces dataset. This confirms that LARR is bias to the white race image over the black race image. It is also observed that, even though the proposed method does not perform as good as LARR, the difference in error is fairly good. Given this observation, we can conclude that the proposed model works fairly well and also generalizes better over LARR.

5 Conclusion

This study is motivated by the rate of inaccuracy reported with age estimation model over black race images. Noting the inefficiency of this existing models in understanding the limitation that comes with underrepresented data, a new dataset is curated using secondary sources. With the newly curated dataset, a hybrid model was proposed and compared to existing state of the art model (LARR). Result show that the proposed methods work well over LARR on Faces, with marginal error on AgeDB and Fair Face.

References

1. Bekhouche, S.E., Ouafi, A., Taleb-Ahmed, A., Hadid, A., Benlamoudi, A.: Facial age estimation using BSIF and LBP. In: International Conference on Electrical Engineering (ICEEB 2014), pp. 1–5 (2014). https://doi.org/10.13140/RG.2.1.1933.6483/1

2. Choi, S.E., Lee, Y.J., Lee, S.J., Park, K.R., Kim, J.: Age estimation using a hierarchical classifier based on global and local facial features. Pattern Recogn. **44**(6), 1262–1281 (2011). https://doi.org/10.1016/j.patcog.2010.12.005

3. Guo, G., Fu, Y., Huang, T.S., Dyer, C.R.: Locally adjusted robust regression for human age estimation. In: 2008 IEEE Workshop on Applications of Computer Vision, WACV (2008). https://doi.org/10.1109/WACV.2008.4544009

4. Karthikeyan, D., Balakrishnan, G.: A comprehensive age estimation on face images using hybrid filter based feature extraction. Biomed. Res. (India) **2018** (2018). https://doi.org/10.4066/biomedicalresearch.29-17-1154

5. Liao, H., Yan, Y., Dai, W., Fan, P.: Age estimation of face images based on CNN and divide-and-rule strategy. Math. Probl. Eng. **2018** (2018). https://doi.org/10.1155/2018/1712686

6. Liu, X., et al.: AgeNet: deeply learned regressor and classifier for robust apparent age estimation. In: Proceedings of the IEEE International Conference on Computer Vision, pp. 258–266, February 2015. https://doi.org/10.1109/ICCVW.2015.42

7. Mittal, S., Agarwal, S., Nigam, M.J.: Real time multiple face recognition: a deep learning approach. In: ACM International Conference Proceeding Series, pp. 70–76 (2018). https://doi.org/10.1145/3299852.3299853

8. Moschoglou, S., Papaioannou, A., Sagonas, C., Deng, J., Kotsia, I., Zafeiriou, S.: AgeDB: the first manually collected, in-the-wild age database. In: IEEE Computer Society Conference on Computer Vision and Pattern Recognition Workshops, July 2017, pp. 1997–2005 (2017). https://doi.org/10.1109/CVPRW.2017.250

9. Nayyar, A.S., Anand Babu, B., Krishnaveni, B., Vaishnavi Devi, M., Gayitri, H.C.: Age estimation: current state and research challenges. J. Med. Sci. (Taiwan) **36**(6), 209–216 (2016). https://doi.org/10.4103/1011-4564.196348

10. Panis, G., Lanitis, A., Tsapatsoulis, N., Cootes, T.F.: Overview of research on facial ageing using the FG-NET ageing database. IET Biom. **5**(2), 37–46 (2016). https://doi.org/10.1049/iet-bmt.2014.0053

11. Rothe, R., Timofte, R., Van Gool, L.: Deep expectation of real and apparent age from a single image without facial landmarks. Int. J. Comput. Vis. **126**(2–4), 144–157 (2016). https://doi.org/10.1007/s11263-016-0940-3

12. Sukhija, P., Behal, S., Singh, P.: Face recognition system using genetic algorithm. Procedia Comput. Sci. **85**(Cms), 410–417 (2016). https://doi.org/10.1016/j.procs.2016.05.183

13. Zhu, Y., Li, Y., Mu, G., Guo, G.: A study on apparent age estimation. In: Proceedings of the IEEE International Conference on Computer Vision, February 2015, pp. 267–273 (2015). https://doi.org/10.1109/ICCVW.2015.43

14. Phulari, R.G.S., Dave, E.J.: Evolution of dental age estimation methods in adults over the years from occlusal wear to more sophisticated recent techniques. Egypt J. Forensic Sci. **11**(36) (2021). https://doi.org/10.1186/s41935-021-00250-6

15. Othmani, A., Taleb, A.R., Abdelkawy, H., Hadid, A.: Age estimation from faces using deep learning: a comparative analysis. Comput. Vis. Image Underst. **196** (2020). https://doi.org/10.1016/j.cviu.2020.102961

16. Li, P., Hu, Y., Wu, X., He, R., Sun, Z.: Deep label refinement for age estimation. Pattern Recogn. **100** (2020). https://doi.org/10.1016/j.patcog.2019.107178

17. Paz Cortés, M.M., Rojo, R., Alía García, E., et al.: Accuracy assessment of dental age estimation with the Willems, Demirjian and Nolla methods in Spanish children: comparative cross-sectional study. BMC Pediatr. **20**, 361 (2020). https://doi.org/10.1186/s12887-020-02247-x

Multi-class Classification of Leaves Using Transfer Learning

Akshay Vaje$^{(\boxtimes)}$, Vaibhav Ranashoor , and Sandip Shingade

Department of Computer Engineering and Information Technology, Veermata Jijabai
Technological Institute (VJTI), Mumbai 400019, MH, India
{amvaje_b17,vvranashoor_b17,stshingade}@it.vjti.ac.in

Abstract. Plants and trees have always played an essential role in the earth's
ecosystem, especially in regulating different biogeochemical cycles that affect
other living creatures. Hence, it is necessary to classify different species of plants
so that valuable species that can help in reducing industrial pollution or provide
medicinal uses to human beings can be identified. Convolutional Neural Network
(CNN) is growing popular and best suited for image recognition and classification. It uses convolutions (a type of filter) of different sizes to detect edges in
an image. Thus, applying these convolutions multiple times on the same images
will output a feature map. However, as the number of layers increase, the size of
CNN model will increase. With an increased CNN model size, the model's latency
to generate an output will also increase. Therefore, in this paper, we have used
Transfer Learning Techniques to drastically reduce the time required to train the
model. Transfer Learning uses pre-train models such as InceptionV3, Resnet50,
VGG16 and then the models are fine-tuned by adding new weights. This paper has
performed a comparative study of these three pretrain models on the Leaf dataset.
A comparative study shows that the VGG16 Transfer Learning model performs
better results than other models.

Keywords: CNN - Convolutional Neural Network · GAN - Generative
Adversarial Networks · DNN - Deep Neural Network

1 Introduction

Leaf image classification has been performed by many researchers. They basically rely
upon customary image classification methods, similar to Scale Invariant Feature Transform (SIFT), Histogram of Oriented Gradients (HOG) and so on These abiding techniques usually work in image classification problems however take much exertion to
choose various sorts of image features for classification, causing researchers to choose
some information and ignoring important information thus reducing the accuracy of
image classification for them [1].

A CNN model may help in reducing the problem with accuracy as discussed above but a large dataset otherwise it may pose an overfitting problem shortly so, we have transfer learning as the solution to training the CNN model with a small dataset. This will help the biologists and others to correctly classify leaf through transfer learning technique.

This paper is all about leaf image classification with higher accuracy using the transfer learning technique. CNN (Convolutional Neural Network) playing a significant role in image classification is way more time-consuming than it seems and requires a large amount of dataset. The paper centres around transfer learning technique that considers previously trained model, e.g., InceptionV3, Resnet50 and VGG16 models then again trains the model using existing weights for a new classification problem. The experiment is conducted on a leaf dataset and the accuracy is compared between different transfer learning models. The paper shows without much knowledge in image processing, the leaf image classification can be achieved with high accuracy using the transfer learning technique with a decrease in time spent in the training process without overfitting on a small dataset [1].

This research investigates leaf image classification and how existing systems put in a lot of work to identify various types of image features for classification. The problem is with the time consumption and larger dataset needed for classification as posed by traditional neural networks, making it difficult for some biologists to form applications able to assist in leaf and plant identification without being accessible all the time.

The use of a previously learnt model on a new problem is known as transfer learning. It's becoming extremely prevalent in deep learning because, it can train deep neural networks with very little data. For example, when training a classifier to predict whether an image contains food, the knowledge gathered during training might be used to recognise drinks, as CNN is not the best choice here due to its high time consumption and extensive use of datasets. This is another problem with CNN that transfer learning solves with lesser data and less time consumption for classification.

2   Related Works

According to [1] the trials done in this study, the transfer learning approach beats the other traditional methods for the specific Flavia data set. The trials were also carried out using a customized data set by the authors. The rate of accuracies is likewise extremely high. They've also demonstrated accuracy testing in enhanced testing data (called as augmented testing data), which replicates real-world usages. Albeit the precision of this plan is reduced by 25% to 30%, they have further developed accuracy by utilizing augmented training data in various structures that are as same as true data as could really be expected.

In a leaf classifier application, this methodology accomplished a higher accuracy percentage, which is reasonable for genuine world use cases in reality (Fig. 1).

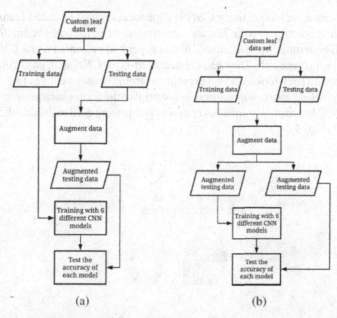

Fig. 1. The process flow of the experiments with the customized dataset. (a) The original training dataset remains unaltered, the labeled testing dataset is modified. (b) Modifications in both the training dataset as well as the testing data [1].

In [2] the researchers involved has trained convolutional neural network with a 25 6 × 6 feature set, a pooling size of 5 layers, and a FC (also known as Fully Connected layer) layer size of 200. On a smartphone called "Samsung Galaxy S4", this model was able to obtain a test error of 60% for top-3 after training and was able to get an average classification score of 17.8 from ImageCLEF, it was also able to classify a single image in 2.5 s [2] (Fig. 2).

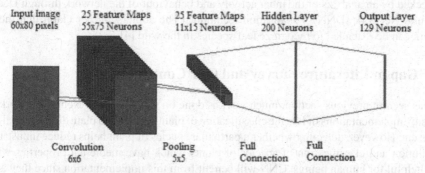

Fig. 2. The convolutional neural network used in paper [2].

The traditional technique using CNN is dependent on a stage called feature extraction; if the methodology used in feature extraction stage is found to be ineffective, the outcome will be wrong [3]. The authors in this paper had presented a new CNN for leaf recognition in this research. They had created a ten-layer CNN with an accuracy rating of 87.92 percent. They looked at this experiment from two perspectives [3].

Secondly, visualisation was utilised to investigate the form characteristic that influences the CNN. In addition, numerous common plants were used to discuss the influence of colour [3] (Fig. 3).

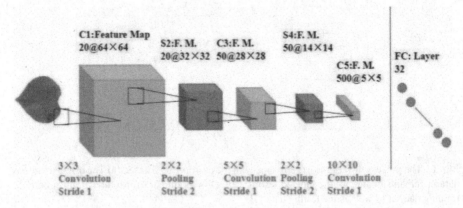

Fig. 3. Network architecture [3]

The author in [4] conducted research on a deep learning approach to learn distinguishing features from photographs of plant/tree leaves with classifiers for leaf species identification. The author justified that CNN's features can better feature leaf images than that hand-crafted features from the experimental results [4]. Moreover, the authors have demonstrated that leaf vein structure is a significant component to recognize diverse species leaves with excellent performance of 99.5%, beating traditional setups. This is checked by an analysis of the inner activity and behaviour of the network through Deep Neural Network (DNN) visualisation technique. The authors further claim that their work can be extended to recognize leaf species in the wild [4].

3   Gap in Literature Survey and Our Contribution

As is seen in previous section, much work is done on Convolutional Neural Networks. Many implementations of it in the classification of plant species and plant disease are also present. However, detecting whether a particular species of plant helps reduce industrial pollution and classification of species of plants which have medicinal properties will be helpful for human beings. CNN will benefit from this implementation since they are better than conventional models, which had been used earlier in machine learning. It will help us identify the species that are useful to humans as herbs or reduce industrial pollution. However, it is yet to be known which CNN model is best for image classification of different leaf species. In this study, we will compare different CNN models with each other and try to obtain the most optimal CNN model that can successfully performs classification of different leaf species with the highest accuracy.

4 Methodology

A. *Dataset*
See Table 1.

Table. 1. A brief overview of all the datasets taken under consideration

Name	Description	Reason for choosing/rejecting dataset
Medicinal Leaf Dataset by Mendeley	The dataset includes thirty different types of healthy medicinal herbs. The dataset contains 1500 photographs of thirty different leaves. Each species contains between 60 and 100 high quality photographs	Reason for choosing the dataset is it contains 30 class/label which will be easy to classify as compared to 100 class/label
Leaf Dataset by UCI machine Learning Repository	The dataset includes 100 different types of leaves. For each species, there are sixteen distinct specimens. The specimens are in Black and White form	Reason for choosing this dataset, it consists of 100 species which we will be using for validating results with another dataset
Leaf Classification Data by Kaggle	There are no groups or labels in this dataset. It's an example of unsupervised learning. The aim of this leaf dataset is to extract features such as form, margin, and texture to accurately classify many plant species	Reason for not choosing the dataset, the dataset doesn't specify any species. It is just a random image dataset arranged in unordered fashion
Leaf snap Dataset	Currently, the dataset includes all 185 tree species found in the North-eastern United States. There are 23147 Lab photographs in the dataset. 7719 Field samples come from the Smithsonian's series of "typical" images	Reason of not choosing the dataset, Since the species is too large it will be very difficult to train the model

4.1 Dataset Chosen

1. We have chosen the medicinal Leaf Dataset by Mendeley Data. The reason for choosing the dataset, it has 30 classes and it is an RGB dataset. Representation of Mendeley leaf dataset can be found in Fig. 4. The dataset consists of 1500 images of 30 different medicinal trees. The process of image augmentation is applied to the Mendeley dataset. For training a CNN model, huge number of data is required and if the size of your data is less, it is recommended to use image augmentation to increase the size of dataset. The image augmentation is applied for both training and testing dataset.

Fig. 4. Example images of Mendeley dataset

2. We have also chosen 100 Leaf Dataset from the UCI Machine Learning repository. Reason for choosing this dataset, it consists of 100 species which we will be used for experiment and comparative analysis with other datasets. Representation of 100 UCI dataset can be found in Fig. 5. The dataset will also be used for validating result with other datasets.

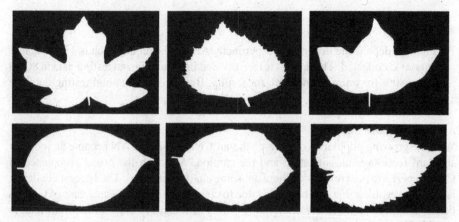

Fig. 5. Example images of 100 Leaf Dataset from UCI ML repository

3. Another dataset Leaf Classification Data by Kaggle and Leaf snap Dataset has more classes/labels. The reason for rejecting the dataset is, classifying a higher number of classes dataset is complicated. The quality of images in the medicinal leaf dataset was also higher than other datasets.

B. Process Flow

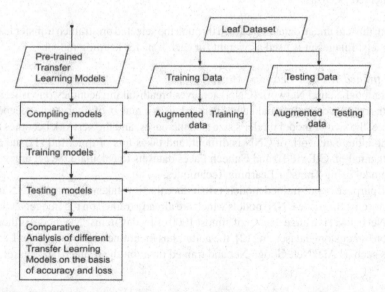

Fig. 6. Process flow of the experiment on the Leaf Dataset using Transfer Learning

The process of classifying leaves are as follows:

1. Figure 6 depicts the flow of our experiment. At first the required dataset i.e., the leaf dataset is collected. The dataset is then divided into training and testing data in 80:20 ratio. 80% for training and 20% for testing. Both the training and testing data use image augmentation.

A) Image Augmentation

With the growing popularity of state-of-the-art CNN models, CNN became an industry standard for image classification and recognition. Although the broad acceptance of CNN to perform different tasks, there are some challenges faced. The biggest challenge is model overfitting that can be caused due to class imbalance. The structure of CNN is dense, and Deep Neural Network requires plenty of images to train, which is difficult to provide [9].

Image Augmentation is a modern technique to improve the diversity of your image data set. Different image augmentation techniques such as traditional transformation, Generative Adversarial Networks (GAN), etc. [10] can apply to create more extensive data sets. The traditional transformation includes modifying the original image and generating a duplicate image based on rotation, mirroring, scaling, shearing, etc. GAN works on two adversarial networks (Generator and discriminator) where one network generates fabricated images, and the discriminator tries to differentiate genuine, and fake images. In this paper, a traditional transformation of image augmentation has been implemented [9, 10].

2. Both the leaf image dataset is passed through the selected pre-trained transfer learning models. ImageNet is used as weight for each transfer learning model.

B) Pre-trained Transfer Learning Models

Convolutional Neural Network (CNN) achieves breath-taking accuracy on visual recognition tasks. As a convolutional neural network uses a matrix of filters to dig deeper into an image, the size of model model's size also increases, and the network becomes bulky. Training a huge network of CNN is difficult and takes lots of time. In [11], the author experimented on CIFAR-10 and Caltech Faces datasets to calculate the accuracy of the CNN model using Transfer Learning Techniques.

The purpose of pre-trained models is to reduce the time taken to train the CNN model. These are custom-made CNN models which are already trained on the ImageNet dataset. ImageNet dataset is a huge dataset of almost 1000 everyday items. The model is then fine-tuned on our custom dataset. In [12], the author has mentioned various transfer Learning models such as AlexNet, GoogleNet and trained them on the Caltech101 dataset.

For this experiment, we have chosen 3 transfer learning model i.e., VGG16, Inception V3 and Resnet50. As per the results in [1], Inception V3 and Resnet50 were the highest performing models and VGG16 model which was introduced by Karen Simonyan and Andrew Zisserman during the ImageNet Challenge in 2014 was the best performing model on ImageNet dataset.

3. The transfer learning model is then fine-tuned with respective datasets. Since, for multiclass classification the class members is greater than 2, softmax activation function is used in the output layer of CNN layer. For Mendeley dataset the output layer will contain 30 layers and for 100 UCI leaf dataset the output layer will contain 100 layers.
4. After adding the output layer, the model is trained. To optimize the model Adam's optimizer is used and the categorical cross-entropy loss was calculated for respective datasets.
5. After training the data, it is then tested on validation set. The model applies all the knowledge gained during the training process and calculates the validation accuracy.
6. At last, a comparative analysis of model on different dataset is performed based on validation loss and accuracy.

5   Experiment and Result

In this experiment, we have used two different datasets. Both the dataset is trained and tested on three transfers learning models, namely VGG16, InceptionV3, and ResNet50. A comparative study is performed, and the best model is selected for an interactive web app.

All the models are implemented on Google Collab. The libraries used to implement this model is TensorFlow and Keras. The image size was (224,224) and all the models are trained for 20 epochs. The batch size for each image is 32.

a. Transfer Learning Models using Mendeley Leaf Dataset

1. Figure 7(a) is the loss and accuracy graph of Mendeley leaf data on InceptionV3 model. The training and validation loss on InceptionV3 model is 0.2996 and 1.8306 respectively while the training and validation accuracy is 96.24% and 89.61% respectively.
2. Figure 7(b) is the loss and accuracy graph of Mendeley leaf data on ResNet50 model. The training and validation loss on ResNet50 model is 1.8123 and 2.1095 respectively while these training and validation accuracy is 64.13% and 66.29% respectively.
3. Figure 7(c) is the loss and accuracy graph of Mendeley leaf data on VGG16 model. The training and validation loss on VGG16 model is 0.0160 and 0.0636 respectively while the training and validation accuracy is 99.63% and 98.63% respectively.

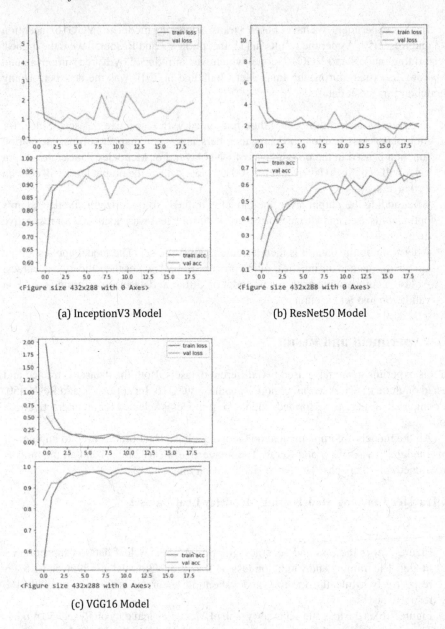

(a) InceptionV3 Model   (b) ResNet50 Model

(c) VGG16 Model

Fig. 7. Training loss, validation loss and training accuracy, validation accuracy of transfer learning models on Mendeley leaf dataset

Table 2. A brief overview of results obtained from Mendeley dataset

Models	Training loss	Validation loss	Training accuracy	Validation accuracy
VGG16	0.0160	0.0636	99.63	98.63
InceptionV3	0.2996	1.8306	96.24	89.61
ResNet50	1.8125	2.1095	64.12	66.29

For validation purposes, our models check another dataset, 100 UCI Leaf dataset.

b. Transfer Learning Models using 100 UCI Leaf Dataset.

1. Figure 8(a) is the loss and accuracy graph of 100 UCI leaf data on InceptionV3 model. The training and validation loss on InceptionV3 model is 2.5316 and 37.7228 respectively while the training and validation accuracy is 92% and 56.08% respectively.
2. Figure 8(b) is the loss and accuracy graph of 100 UCI leaf data on ResNet50 model. The training and validation loss on ResNet50 model is 4.0433 and
3. 17.0019 respectively while the training and validation accuracy is 64.56% and 36.36% respectively
4. Figure 8(c) is the loss and accuracy graph of 100 UCI leaf data on VGG16 model. The training and validation loss on VGG16 model is 0.2272 and 4.5427 respectively while the training and validation accuracy is 94.55% and 59.16% respectively.

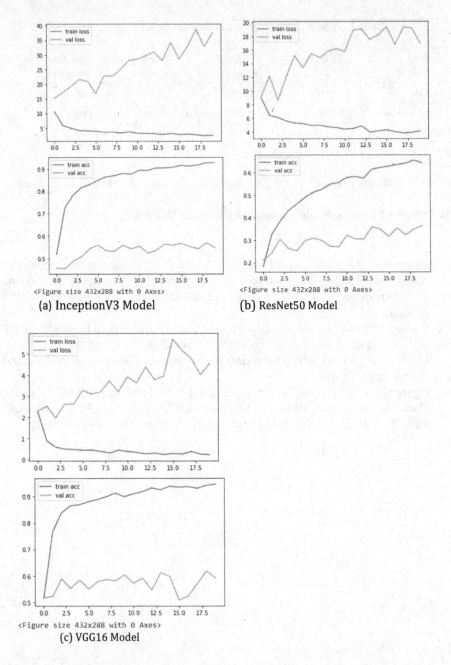

(a) InceptionV3 Model

(b) ResNet50 Model

(c) VGG16 Model

Fig. 8. Training loss, validation loss and training accuracy, validation accuracy of all 3 transfer learning models on 100 UCI leaf dataset

Table 3. A brief overview of results obtained from UCI leaf dataset.

Models	Training loss	Validation loss	Training accuracy	Validation accuracy
VGG16	0.2272	4.5427	94.55	59.16
InceptionV3	2.5316	37.7228	92	56.08
ResNet50	4.0433	17.0019	64.56	33.36

6 Conclusion

Transfer Learning is a proven state of the art method for leaf image classification and achieves higher accuracy. In this experiment, three Transfer Learning models namely VGG16, InceptionV3 and ResNet50 were introduced. These models were trained on two datasets namely Mendeley Leaf Dataset and 100 UCI Leaf Dataset. The results for respective dataset can be found in Table 2 and Table 3. According to the results, validation accuracy of VGG16 on Mendeley dataset is 98.63% and on 100 UCI leaf dataset is 59.16% which is higher than InceptionV3 and Resnet50. The evaluation is based on testing accuracy score. After the result analysis, the VGG16 model was integrated with a web application using a flask, which predicted output after feeding leaf image as input.

The above experiment is a sequential implementation of Multiclass Classification of Leaves using Transfer Learning. Thus, the future work would be to implement multiclass classification of leaves based on Parallel processing techniques.

References

1. Esmaeili, H., Phoka, T.: Transfer learning for leaf classification with convolutional neural networks. In: 2018 15th International Joint Conference on Computer Science and Software Engineering (JCSSE). IEEE (2018)
2. Jassmann, T.J., Tashakkori, R., Mitchell Parry, R.: Leaf classification utilizing a convolutional neural network. In: SoutheastCon 2015. IEEE (2015)
3. Liu, J., et al.: Plant leaf classification based on deep learning. In: 2018 Chinese Automation Congress (CAC). IEEE (2018)
4. Lee, S.H., et al.: Deep-plant: plant identification with convolutional neural networks. In: 2015 IEEE International Conference on Image Processing (ICIP). IEEE (2015)
5. Lorente, O., Riera, I., Rana. A.: Image classification with classic and deep learning techniques (2021)
6. Szegedy, C., Vanhoucke, V., Ioffe, S., Shlens, J., Wojna, Z.: Rethinking the inception architecture for computer vision. In: IEEE 2016 IEEE Conference on Computer Vision and Pattern Recognition (CVPR) - Las Vegas, NV, USA, 27 June 2016–30 June 2016. 2016 IEEE Conference on Computer Vision and Pattern Recognition (CVPR), pp. 2818–2826 (2016). https://doi.org/10.1109/CVPR.2016.308
7. Tammina, S.: Transfer learning using VGG-16 with deep convolutional neural network for classifying images. Int. J. Sci. Res. Publ. (IJSRP) **9**, 9420 (2019). https://doi.org/10.29322/IJSRP.9.10.2019.p9420

8. He, K., Zhang, X., Ren, S., Sun, J.: Deep residual learning for image recognition. In: 2016 IEEE Conference on Computer Vision and Pattern Recognition (CVPR), p. 770778 (2016). https://doi.org/10.1109/CVPR.2016.90
9. Mikolajczyk, A., Grochowski, M.: Data augmentation for improving deep learning in image classification problem. In: 2018 International Interdisciplinary PhD Workshop (IIPhDW), pp. 117–122 (2018). https://doi.org/10.1109/IIPHDW.2018.8388338
10. Wang, J., Perez, L.: The effectiveness of data augmentation in image classification using deep learning, Technical report (2017)
11. Hussain, M., Bird, J., Faria, D.: A study on CNN transfer learning for image classification (2018)
12. Zabir, M., Fazira, N., Ibrahim, Z., Sabri, N.: Evaluation of pre-trained convolutional neural network models for object recognition. Int. J. Eng. Technol. (UAE) **7**, 95–98 (2018). https://doi.org/10.14419/ijet.v7i3.15.17509

Author Index

Printed in the United States
by Baker & Taylor Publisher Services

Printed in the United States
by Baker & Taylor Publisher Services